OXFORD BUSINESS ENGLISH SKILLS

Effective

SOCIALIZING

JEREMY COMFORT

with YORK ASSOCIATES

No. Sang Loon

OXFORD UNIVERSITY PRESS 1997

Oxford University Press,
Great Clarendon Street, Oxford OX2 6DP

Oxford New York
Athens Auckland Bangkok Bombay
Calcutta Cape Town Dar es Salaam Delhi
Florence Hong Kong Istanbul Karachi
Kuala Lumpur Madras Madrid Melbourne
Mexico City Nairobi Paris Singapore
Taipei Tokyo Toronto

and associated companies in
Berlin Ibadan

Oxford and *Oxford English*
are trade marks of Oxford University Press

ISBN 0 19 457096 7

© Oxford University Press

First published 1997

Acknowledgements

Illustrations by Nigel Paige
Photography by Paul Freestone
Cover illustration by Adam Willis

Typeset in ITC Franklin Gothic
and Adobe Minion

Printed in Hong Kong

Contents

Introduction
page 4

Who's who in *Effective Socializing*
page 7

Unit		Communication skills	Language knowledge	Socializing practice
1	**First contact** page 8	welcoming a visitor	introductions opening small talk	first meetings
2	**Getting to know each other** page 14	effective question and answer techniques	asking and responding to questions	developing conversation
3	**More contacts** page 20	everyday meetings inclusive behaviour	greetings, requests, favours, small talk	everyday meetings
4	**Arrangements** page 26	understanding and responding to invitations	inviting, accepting, declining, offering, refusing	making arrangements
5	**Arriving for dinner** page 32	hosting: time, dress, gifts	thanking, offering, and responding	welcoming and entertaining guests
6	**Dinner** page 38	complimenting inclusive behaviour	showing appreciation, offering opinions, comments	stimulating discussion
7	**After work** page 44	choosing and developing topics of conversation	structuring and developing conversation	conversation topics
8	**Farewells** page 50	wishing farewell	leaving, farewells, reinforcing contacts	saying goodbye

Listening Tapescript
page 55

Answer Key
page 68

Video Transcript
page 81

Introduction

Introduction to the course

Learners of Business English often feel their language and skills are most exposed in social situations. Whether they are hosts, guests, or just colleagues meeting after work, they will be able to communicate more effectively if they feel at ease. They need to be able to relax when using English, and to acquire the necessary language and communication skills to express their thoughts and feelings appropriately.

Effective Socializing is a practical and accessible course specifically designed to equip learners with these essential skills. It is divided into eight units which deal progressively with key aspects of socializing from first introductions and conversation-building, through to developing contacts, and farewells. The course aims to build competence in a variety of contexts, so that by the end of their period of study learners will have confidence in their ability to handle most social situations.

Course components

The course consists of four components: a video, a Student's Book, an audio cassette, and a Teacher's Book.

The Video

The video is the central component of the course. It contains approximately 25 minutes of sample social situations. Based around the story of two foreign visitors to Britain, it illustrates the key social situations they encounter: first contacts, getting to know each other, making arrangements, dining out, after work drinks, and final farewells. The video acts as a focus for all the activities contained in the Student's Book.

The Student's Book

The book consists of eight units which correspond to those in the video. Each unit is divided into three sections: *Communication skills*, *Language knowledge*, and *Socializing practice*.

The *Communication skills* section identifies and practises key socializing skills which are illustrated on the video, and aims to involve the learner in a process of feedback, evaluation, and development. The *Language knowledge* section, supported by the audio cassette, focuses on and expands the learner's knowledge in key functional and lexical areas. It also deals with the impact of culture on social interaction by looking at areas such as physical contact, ways of addressing people, and time.

The *Socializing practice* section gives the learner the opportunity to put both communication skills and language knowledge into practice using a variety of role-plays and simulations.

The Audio Cassette   This consists of extracts from additional social situations and forms the basis of listening activities in the *Language knowledge* section of the Student's Book.

The Teacher's Book   This book provides an introduction to the course from the teacher's point of view. It is intended as a guide to help the teacher to handle the different components of the course most effectively. It offers suggestions for further exploitation in the classroom and self-study time, and contains extra, photocopiable materials for socializing practice.

The approach

In each unit, *Effective Socializing* first illustrates a poor model of behaviour in a social setting in order to demonstrate what can go wrong (Version 1). Often the responsibility for things going badly is shared between both host and guest. The course then moves on to look at a good model in which the speakers communicate successfully (Version 2). The video is essential as the starting point for each unit.

The approach is designed to develop learners' abilities in two main areas:

Communication skills   The course develops the key skills of communicating positively and appropriately in social situations. It seeks to build the learners' confidence in their ability to deal with these situations. Skills such as handling visitors, building relationships, developing conversations, and responding positively are demonstrated on the video. These are then analysed and practised with the support of the Student's Book.

Language knowledge   Language areas such as introductions, offers, small talk, and asking and responding to questions are presented and practised in the Student's Book. Additional exercises seek to develop the learners' vocabulary around a range of topics for social conversation. The audio cassette is used to further illustrate and practise these areas. At the end of this section there is a short text dealing with the impact of culture on social interaction: these texts are intended as a basis for discussion and the development of cultural awareness.

Using the course

All parts of the course are designed to work either as classroom material or for self-study.

In the classroom

Each unit takes the learner through the objectives in the areas of *Communication skills*, *Language knowledge*, and *Socializing practice*. There is an introduction designed to make the learners reflect on their own experiences, and to anticipate the focus of the material which follows. Depending on the needs of the group or the amount of time available, the course can either be followed from start to finish, or learners can concentrate on selected units. The *Socializing practice* activities in the Student's Book provide relevant, context-based practice of the key aspects of the unit. These activities are designed for either pairs or small groups. Wherever possible, they should be recorded on audio cassette to enable both teacher and learners to analyse and correct the learner's performance when the tape is played back.

Self-study

The video-based activities focusing on communication skills have been developed with the classroom in mind. However, most of the questions have answers in the Answer Key, and individuals can use the video on a self-access basis. The *Language knowledge* section can certainly be usefully followed as self-study. The *Socializing practice* section necessarily involves pair or group work, although preparation for these activities could also be done during self-study time.

Who's who in *Effective Socializing*

Effective Socializing illustrates a series of encounters between two foreign visitors and members of the Marketing Department of Tectron UK.

The company

TECTRON UK

Tectron UK is a British-owned engineering company which produces sophisticated computer applications for the manufacturing sector. Its headquarters are in Harlow, to the north-east of London. It has subsidiaries in France, Spain, and Ireland, and a large research and development centre in Copenhagen. It currently employs a total of 950 people worldwide, and there are plans to expand into Latin America and South East Asia in the near future.

The guests

Maria de Miguel
Maria is a management trainee from Tectron España. She has come to the UK on a six-month secondment to Tectron UK. She is attached to Peter's department and will be working quite closely with Paula.

Jens Foss
Jens is an engineer from Tectron's Danish subsidiary in Copenhagen. He is visiting Tectron UK for a few days acting as a consultant. He is in his late thirties, and has two young children.

The hosts

Peter O'Donnell
Peter is the Marketing Manager of Tectron UK. He is aged about fifty-five, and is a little formal in his style of communication. He is married to Daphne. They have a son and a daughter, both in their twenties.

Paula Field
Paula is a Marketing Assistant who reports to Peter O'Donnell. She is about thirty years old. She is usually quite informal and friendly, although she can sometimes come across as rather officious and abrupt.

Daphne O'Donnell
Daphne is in her early fifties. She has her own career, but often has to help entertain her husband Peter's customers and colleagues.

1 First contact

Objectives

Communication skills	welcoming a visitor
Language knowledge	introductions, opening small talk
Socializing practice	first meetings

Communication skills

Pre-viewing

1   What do you do and say when you meet someone for the first time? How important are the first two or three minutes of these opening contacts?

2   Read the Video Socializing Context.

Video Socializing Context

The people

Peter O'Donnell
is the Marketing Manager of Tectron UK.

Paula Field
is a Marketing Assistant. She reports to Peter.

Maria de Miguel
is a management trainee from Tectron España. She has arrived for a six-month work placement with Tectron UK.

The situation

Peter and Paula are just finishing a morning meeting. Maria arrives at reception, and is directed to Peter's office.

Viewing

▶ 3   Watch Version 1 with the sound down. What do you notice about the behaviour of the three characters? What sort of welcome does Maria get?

▶ 4   Watch Version 1 with the sound up. What does Maria expect to happen? How do you think Peter handles this first contact with Maria?

▶ 5   Watch Version 2 with the sound down. What differences are there in the behaviour of the three characters?

▶ **6** Now watch Version 2 with the sound up. List the things Peter does more effectively. How do you think Maria will feel after this first contact with Peter and Paula?

▭ **7** Listen to a number of people talking about first meetings in their country. Make notes under the headings below:

Extract	importance of socializing	physical contact	names	opening small talk
one	_____	_____	_____	_____
two	_____	_____	_____	_____
three	_____	_____	_____	_____
four	_____	_____	_____	_____

Discuss the above aspects of first meetings. Which countries do you think the people come from? How do people behave in this situation in your country?

Language knowledge

PETER 'Hello, you must be Maria. I'm Peter O'Donnell. Welcome to Tectron UK.'
MARIA 'Thank you. It's good to be here.'

▭ **1** Listen to these extracts from first meetings. For each extract, decide whether it is formal or informal, and business or pleasure.

Extract	formal / informal	business / pleasure
one	_____	_____
two	_____	_____
three	_____	_____
four	_____	_____

Language focus Welcoming visitors

Welcoming

Welcome to . . .
It's a (great) *pleasure to welcome you to . . .* (F)
On behalf of . . . I'd like to welcome you to . . . (F)

Introducing yourself

My name's . . . I'm . . . (job / position)
Let me introduce myself. I'm . . .
How do you do. My name's . . . (F)
We haven't met. I'm . . .

Introducing someone else

I'd like to introduce you to . . . (F)
Have you met . . . ?
. . . , this is . . .

Responding to introductions

How do you do. My name's . . . (F)
Nice to meet you. Mine's . . .

Offering

Let me get you a coffee.
Would you like a coffee?
Let me take your coat.

NOTE
The expressions marked (F) are used in more formal situations. When welcoming visitors, the level of formality will depend mostly on the culture of the country you live in, and also on the type of organization you work for. In the UK, it is becoming more usual to adopt a more informal style of communication.

Small talk topics

Travel

How was your trip?
Did you have any trouble finding us?

It was fine / very smooth / easy.
It was a bit delayed / the traffic was terrible / it was a bit rough.
I missed my connection / the plane was late.
There were no problems.

Accommodation

How's your hotel?
Is everything all right?

It's very comfortable / convenient / luxurious.
The service is excellent.
It's rather noisy / dirty.
The service is rather slow.
The rooms are a bit cramped.

Weather

How do you find the weather here?
What was it like when you left?

It's lovely / sunny / warm.
It was dismal / cloudy / cold / damp / wet / stormy / windy.

NOTE
We often modify our negative remarks by using words like *a little, a bit,* or *rather.* When we insert these words, our remarks are softened. They become less direct and sound more natural.

 2 Listen to these five introductions. How do you think they continued? Choose from the responses below.

   a Nice to meet you. I'm Sarah Sarandon, Vice-President, Marketing.
   b Thank you. It's a pleasure to be here.
   c Not really. I guess we've never met. My name's John Dunn.
   d How do you do. I'm Tania Philips.
   e No, I haven't. Why don't you introduce me?

3 Make appropriate introductions in the following situations.

    a You are at a company party. You see the new head of marketing who you would like to meet. Introduce yourself.

    b You have just arrived at a restaurant. Your partner hasn't met your colleagues. Introduce them.

    c Welcome a new member of staff to your department and then introduce him / her to your colleagues.

    d At an informal lunch, introduce yourself to the daughter of a colleague.

    e Introduce yourself to the new head of your business unit.

4 Match the opening small talk questions about travel, accommodation, and the weather (1–10) with the most appropriate response (a–j). Then listen to the correct combinations to confirm your answers.

    1 What was the weather like when you left?
    2 How do you find the weather?
    3 I suppose this weather must be a bit of a shock to you.
    4 How was your trip?
    5 Did you have any trouble finding us?
    6 Did you get in on time?
    7 How's the hotel?
    8 Did you find somewhere to stay?
    9 Have you got a room with a view?
   10 How was the crossing?

    a Just a little bit late.
    b Fine. Everything went smoothly, thank you.
    c Pretty cold. It was only four degrees when I left home.
    d Not yet. Could you recommend somewhere?
    e No problems at all. The map you sent me was excellent.
    f A bit rough but not too bad.
    g It is a bit. It was below zero back in the States.
    h Lovely. Sunny skies. Nice and warm.
    i Unfortunately not. All I can see is the factory opposite.
    j Very comfortable, thank you.

5 Modify the remarks below to make them softer or less direct.

    a It's cold.
    b The room's filthy.
    c The view's awful.
    d The crossing was rough.
    e The traffic was slow.
    f The weather's disappointing.

6 Pair work – speeding up your responses

a

Imagine you are being met at an airport by Student B. Respond appropriately to his / her questions and comments.

Student B

Imagine you are meeting Student A off a plane (use his / her real name). Ask the following questions and make the following comments. Student A should respond appropriately.

1 Hello . . . (his / her name). I'm . . . (your name). Nice to meet you.
2 Let me take your case.
3 How was the trip?
4 Just a moment, I've got to pay for the parking.
5 So what do you think of our weather?
6 What was it like in your part of the world?
7 I thought we'd drive to your hotel first.
8 We've booked you into the Holiday Inn.
9 I expect you're tired after the journey.
10 I'll pick you up in a couple of hours and we'll go out to dinner.

b

Student A

Imagine you have just met a new colleague, Student B. You have accompanied him / her to a party. He / she should respond appropriately to the following questions.

1 Would you like me to introduce you to some colleagues?
2 Have you met Anna Howard?
3 Let me introduce you to my old friend, Charles Digby. Charles, this is . . .
4 How was the weather back home?
5 Where are you staying?
6 Have you got a reasonable room?
7 What about your trip?
8 Did you fly?
9 Oh look. There's Kerry Fisher. Would you like me to introduce you to her?
10 How long are you going to be here for?

Student B

Imagine you are at a party. Student A is looking after you. Respond appropriately to his / her comments and questions.

Names and titles | *Culture note*

The Americans are famous for their early use of first names in any relationship, however formal. You sometimes notice how Americans repeat your name frequently in the first five minutes of conversation. The British also use first names most of the time. However, they are not so good at remembering names and will frequently use no name at all! In some cultures it is important to address someone using their title – for example Doctor, Professor, etc. In both British and American cultures we tend not to use titles. In fact, in an effort to be completely egalitarian, we often avoid the title Mrs, which indicates a woman is married. Instead, the title Ms (pronounced 'muz') is preferred. This is also frequently used in written correspondence.

Discuss how you address colleagues, customers, bosses, friends, and family in your culture.

Socializing practice

Pair work 1

Modify the dialogue below to make it more formal and less direct.

A: Welcome to A & T. I'm Johan Petersson. I look after the factory here.
B: Nice to meet you. My name's Susan Parkes.
A: Nice to meet you, Susan. How was your trip?
B: Slow. I got caught in awful traffic.
A: Sorry to hear that. Anyway, have you checked in?
B: Yes.
A: Everything OK?
B: Fine.
A: So how do you find our weather?
B: It's hot. When I left home, it was only ten degrees.

Pair work 2

Script a dialogue for a welcome scene which would be typical in your workplace. After you have scripted it, try recording it on tape.

Group work

Imagine you are all invited to a formal business reception. At this reception, you have the following objectives:

1 to introduce yourself to everyone
2 to engage in a minimum of one minute's small talk
3 to learn something about each person you meet

Prepare yourself by:

1 giving yourself an identity – name, job, background
2 establishing your current situation – live here / visiting / working, etc.
3 preparing some small talk – weather, travel, etc.

2 Getting to know each other

Objectives

Communication skills	effective question and answer techniques
Language knowledge	asking and responding to questions
Socializing practice	developing conversation

Communication skills

Pre-viewing

1 What sort of questions do you ask someone when you are getting to know them? What subjects do people normally talk about in the early stages of getting to know someone?

2 Read the Video Socializing Context.

Video Socializing Context

The people

Maria Miguel
is a management trainee from Tectron España.

Peter O'Donnell
is Marketing Manager of Tectron UK.

Paula Field
is a Marketing Assistant with Tectron UK

The situation

Peter O'Donnell has suggested that he, Maria, and Paula meet for lunch at the local wine bar. Paula and Maria have arrived. Peter is late.

Viewing

3 Watch Version 1 with the sound down. What can you tell from watching the body language of Paula and Maria?

4 Watch Version 1 with the sound up. What questions does Paula ask Maria? What sort of answers does Maria give? What do you think of the choice of topics for conversation?

5 Watch Version 2 with the sound down. What signs are there that the communication is more successful?

6 Watch Version 2 with the sound up. Focus on Maria's responses to Paula's questions. What differences do you notice compared to Version 1 ?

7 **Pair work**

You have both arrived by plane for a meeting. You have not met before. You have been met by a driver who has left you for a few minutes while he goes to pick up the car. Prepare for three minutes of small talk with each other. When you are both ready, record your conversation. Play it back to check how natural it sounds.

Language knowledge

PAULA ' *Was it? I'm sure it's not normally this cold.* '
MARIA ' *Still, it's warmer than I expected.* '
PAULA ' *Really! I suppose it's still pretty hot in Spain at this time of year.* '

1 Listen to some extracts of people making small talk. Decide whether the dialogues are successful or not. If they are successful, what topic produces some common ground?

Extract	successful / unsuccessful	topic / common ground
one	_____	_____
two	_____	_____
three	_____	_____
four	_____	_____

MY BOSS SAID HE HAD DONE BUSINESS WITH YOU BEFORE AND SUGGESTED THIS CHEAP RESTAURANT

Language focus Question types

The initiator of small talk always hopes that his or her questions will elicit more than a one- or two-word answer. You need to have a number of questions available in order to find a topic that develops into an interesting conversation.

For a conversation to develop positively, the responder in any small talk exchange needs to give full answers. If possible, these should include a comment (see the extracts in **1** above).

Closed (these questions elicit Yes / No answers, and may be not very effective)

Did you see that film on television?
Do you live near here?
Have you been here long?

Open (these questions should elicit a fuller answer)

What about the country?
Where do you spend your holidays?

Statement (expressed to encourage a reaction)

I don't like working late.
We work a flexitime system here.
Starting later in the morning suits me.

Reactions

Yes, I agree.
Really?
That's interesting.
Me too.

Reflections

So you think . . . ?
I suppose you are . . . ?

Topics

Jobs

Quite a lot of opening small talk centres around people's jobs. Most of us classify people initially in terms of their work.

What do you do?
  I'm a teacher / engineer / lawyer. (profession)
  I work for the ABC Corporation. (employer)
  I work for myself at the moment. (self-employed)
  I look after the children. / I'm a housewife / husband.

What line are you in?
  I'm in computing. (industry)
  I'm in marketing. (function)

How long have you been with them?
Do you like it? / Are they a good employer? / Is the job interesting? (more personal questions)
How's business?

Family

Are you married?
What does your wife / husband do?
Do you have any children?
How old are they?
Are they at school / at college / working?
Do they still live at home?

Spare time

What do you in the evenings / at weekends?
Where do you spend your holidays?
What do you do in your spare time?
Do you like films / gardening / walking / sport?

Origins

Where do you come from?
Where were you brought up?
How young were you when you moved to . . . ?
Which part of . . . were you born in?

2 Listen to these questions. In each case, try to answer the question and then make a comment or add some more information.

For example:

'*How long have you been working?*' (question)
'*Not so long – about five years.*' (answer)
'*Long enough, really!*' (comment)
'*Before that I was studying.*' (add information)

Now compare your responses with the sample exchanges.

3 Pair work

Practise asking and answering questions on these topics. Follow the same pattern as in exercise **2**.

– jobs
– family
– spare time
– origins
– any other topics which interest you

4

Taboos	*Culture note*

Some topics may be considered taboo in some cultures. In the UK, many people avoid the topic of religion. This may be because Britain is now a very secular country where religion has a relatively minor role, or it may be that we regard someone's religious beliefs as very personal. A stereotype of the Americans is that they ask you how much money you earn quite soon after meeting you. This is certainly not generally true. However, Americans do tend to be more open about money and its importance. Death is a taboo subject in many cultures; people seem to be ill at ease discussing anything connected with the end of their lives! Politics can be a delicate subject in some parts of the world. In the UK, many people are very guarded about their political allegiance.

Discuss which subjects are taboo in your country, and the reasons which lie behind these taboos.

Socializing practice

Pair work

Working in pairs, share out the roles below. Read the situation and prepare your role. Then act it out. If possible, record the conversation to check that you have used appropriate language.

Situation

You both work for Sintra Telecom but have not met before. You have been called to a meeting. You each arrive to find just one colleague present. You need to get to know each other. Try to find something you have in common.

Student A

You are in Information Technology. You work for the Brazilian subsidiary. You are visiting Europe to learn more about the IT systems used in European subsidiaries. You were born in Lisbon, Portugal and were brought up in Brazil. You studied Computer Science at Stanford University in America. You are married with two children. You love sport; you play tennis and golf; you watch as much football as possible. You are no longer so interested in music, although when you were younger, you played electric guitar in a pop group.

Student B

You are in sales. You work at the headquarters of Sintra Telecom in the UK. You were born in Scotland but brought up in the south of England. You studied economics at university. You are not married but you live with your partner. In your spare time, you go to the cinema a lot, sometimes to the theatre. You love music, especially opera. You are not very interested in sport. When you were younger, you used to be the drummer in a rock band.

Group work 1

In groups of three, read the situation and choose a role. Act out the role-play and record it if possible. Try to find something you all have in common.

Situation

You have all been visiting an electronics trade fair in Florida. You are sitting at a bar, waiting for taxis to take you to the airport. Use the time while you are waiting to get to know each other. Act out the role-play in real time (watch the clock for your taxis).

Student A

You are an Export Manager for a software development company. This is the first time you have visited the trade fair and you found it very disappointing – a waste of time. You come from Lyons in France. You were born and brought up there. You are married with three children. You are interested in computers. You have your own multimedia equipment where you develop programs. You also love travelling and are planning to visit New Zealand this summer. Your taxi should arrive in about ten minutes. Your plane for Paris leaves in one and a half hours.

You are the Marketing Manager of a computer company. You have visited this trade fair many times. You found the exhibits more interesting than usual. You were born in Florence, Italy. You were brought up there but went to university in Milan. You have always worked in the computer industry but personally you are not very interested in computers! You are not married. In your spare time you do a lot of sailing. This summer you will be sailing in the Aegean. You are catching the plane to Paris in about an hour and half. You have ordered a taxi to arrive in about ten minutes.

Student C

You are an electronics engineer working for a software development company. You have been sent to this trade fair to look at developments in virtual reality. You found the trade fair a big disappointment – nothing really worth seeing. You come from Ireland. You were born and brought up in Cork in the south-west of Ireland. You have recently got married and your wife is expecting your first baby. Your main interest is in music; you play the violin in local folk group. This summer you are staying at home, working on renovating part of your house. You are catching a plane to Paris and then catching a connecting flight to Dublin. You have ordered a taxi to arrive in about fifteen minutes.

Group work 2

Working in groups of three or four participants, imagine that you have all met for the first time. You are all waiting for a taxi to take you to a conference hotel. Use the time to get to know each other.

3 More contacts

Objectives

Communication skills	everyday meetings, inclusive behaviour
Language knowledge	greetings, requests, favours, small talk
Socializing practice	everyday meetings

Communication skills

Pre-viewing

1 What do you do and say when you meet a colleague first thing in the morning?
How important is it to make contact with your colleagues on a daily basis?

2 Read the Video Socializing Context.

Video Socializing Context

The people

Paula Field
is a Marketing Assistant with Tectron UK.

Maria de Miguel
is a management trainee from Tectron España.

Jens Foss
is a Danish engineer, visiting Tectron UK for a few days.

The situation

Paula has gone down to reception to meet Jens. While she's there, Maria arrives for work.

Viewing

▶ 3 Watch Version 1. How do you think Paula behaves towards Maria and Jens? What should she have done differently?

▶ 4 Watch Version 1 again. Identify the following moments:
a Paula indicates she is not interested in chatting to Maria *7.16*
b Paula gives Jens an abrupt welcome *7.28*
c Paula asks Maria to do her a favour *7.23*
d Maria and Jens have to introduce themselves *7.44*

▶ 5 Watch Version 2 with the sound down. What differences are there in the body language of the three characters?

6 Watch Version 2 again with the sound up. Focus on these moments:

  a Paula engages Maria in some friendly small talk
  b Paula includes Jens and Maria
  c Paula pays attention to Jens

Post-viewing

7 In daily contacts with colleagues and friends, how do you behave? What advice would you give a visitor to your country concerning the following aspects of body language?

  – eye contact
  – physical distance (between each other)
  – facial expression
  – physical contact (handshakes, hugs, kisses, etc.)
  – stance or posture (hands in pockets, sitting, standing)

Language knowledge

PAULA '*Jens, would you mind signing in before we go upstairs?*'

1 Listen to these three extracts. In each case, say what is requested and if the response is positive or cautious.

Extract	request	response
one	_____	_____
two	_____	_____
three	_____	_____

HALLO, WE HAVEN'T MET. MY NAME'S HAROLD AND THIS IS MY ASSISTANT GARY.

Language focus Greetings and requests

Greetings

Hello. / Hi. / Good morning. / Good afternoon.
How are you?
How are things?
Nice to see you again. (after a long gap)

Responses

Fine, and you?
Not so bad. How are you?

NOTE
The greeting 'How are you?' is normally part of a ritual. We don't expect people to reply honestly or in detail. Therefore, in most situations, we don't respond by saying 'Not so well' or 'Awful'. Clearly these responses would involve further enquiries!

Requests (favours)

I wondered if you could . . .
Would you mind . . . -ing . . . ?
Could you . . . ?
I've got a favour to ask you. Could you . . . ?

NOTE
The language we use for making a request will depend on the nature of the request, and who we are asking. Normally, we would use more formal or polite language for difficult or more personal requests, especially with someone we don't know well. For smaller requests, or with people we know well, we are usually less formal.

Responses

Sure. / Certainly.
Not at all. / It'd be a pleasure.
I suppose so.
Well . . . that's not so easy / a bit of a problem.
We often ask people to lend us something. Be careful how you use *lend* and *borrow*:
   'Could you lend me 10p for the phone?'
   'I wonder if I could borrow your copy of the agenda?'

When we respond positively to a request we say *'No'*:
   'Would you mind postponing the meeting?'
   'No, not at all. / No, that's all right.'

When we respond negatively we tend not to say
   'Yes (I do mind)*'*:
   'Would you mind cancelling the meeting?'
   'Well, I'm not sure . . .'

---

2 Listen and complete the dialogues.

a

A: Hi, Marion. How are things?

B: _____?

A: Fine thanks. _____ ask you a favour?

B: _____

A: Could I borrow your laptop for the weekend?

B: _____ I'll bring it in tomorrow.

A: Thanks, Marion. That's really good of you.

b

A: Morning, Tom. How are you?

B: _____?

A: Actually, I'm feeling a bit rough.

B: Oh, I'm sorry to hear that.

A: _____ a couple of aspirin?

B: Umm _____ Why don't you try Jonathan? He's a walking medical chest.

A: Good idea. See you later.

B: Bye. Hope you feel better soon.

c

A: Hello. How are you doing?

B: Hello. _____

A: Fine thanks. Actually, I'm glad I bumped into you.

B: Why's that?

A: Well, _____ I missed the meeting this afternoon?

B: _____

A: You see, I've got to pick up my son from the doctor's.

B: If you have to, _____

A: Thanks very much.

3   Pair work

Greet each other and make the following requests. Remember to use language that is appropriate to the nature of the request, and to your relationship with the other person.

a   borrow some change for coffee
b   have a day off (holiday)
c   leave work early
d   sign a letter
e   start a meeting early
f   attend a two-day training course
g   use the other person's office for a meeting
h   book some extra holiday over Christmas

4 | **Physical contact**

In social contact with people from other cultures, it is sometimes very difficult to know how to behave.

handshakes	On what occasions do you shake hands? Who do you shake hands with? Should the handshake be firm and brief, or long and warm?
kissing	Do you ever kiss anyone outside intimate relationships? If yes, who do you kiss? How many kisses do you give someone?
touching	Do you ever touch each other? Who can you touch? In what way is it acceptable to touch someone?
proximity	Do you stand / sit close to people, or do you keep your distance?

Discuss the above questions and any other aspects of physical contact which are relevant to your own culture.

Socializing practice

Pair work 1 speeding up your responses

Student A
Greet Student B and / or make requests in the following situations.

Student B
Respond appropriately.

a You meet a colleague in the corridor.
b You need some change to make a telephone call.
c You need some help with checking the English in a fax.
d It's raining and you would like to borrow an umbrella.
e You want to open a conversation with a colleague over lunch in the canteen.
f You would like a customer to confirm details of an arrangement by fax.
g You would like to ask your boss if you can finish work early today.
h You greet a colleague you haven't seen for a long time.
i You would like to ask a personal favour of a colleague.
j You would like one of your team to finish a job this evening. It means working late.

Pair work 2 speeding up your responses

Student B

Greet Student A and / or make requests in the following situations.

Student A

Respond appropriately.

a   You meet a colleague first thing in the morning.
b   You meet a colleague who you haven't seen for a long time.
c   You need some change for the parking meter.
d   You need to use a colleague's phone to make a personal call.
e   You meet a friend on the way into work.
f   You need a lift home as your car is being repaired.
g   You are staying in a conference hotel. You have forgotten
     your toothpaste.
h   You need to leave a meeting early to catch a train.
i   You would like to speak to a colleague privately before the end
     of the day.
j   You would like to ask a colleague a personal favour.

Pair work 3

Work in pairs. You will meet each other on the way in to work. Prepare a
request you would like to make of your colleague: for example, a request
about work (meetings, reports, letters, etc.), a request to borrow
something (office, computer, car, etc.), a request about home life (time off
for the family, etc.).

Record the conversation. Then play it back to check that you have used
appropriate language.

Arrangements

Objectives

Communication skills	understanding and responding to invitations
Language knowledge	inviting, accepting, declining, offering, refusing
Socializing practice	making arrangements

Communication skills

Pre-viewing

1 When you have visitors (colleagues, customers, etc.), do you invite them out in the evening? If so, where do you invite them – to your home, to a restaurant, or somewhere else? How formal are these occasions?

2 Read the Video Socializing Context.

Video Socializing Context

The people

Peter O'Donnell
is the Marketing Manager of Tectron UK.

Maria de Miguel
is a management trainee from Tectron España.

Jens Foss
is a Danish engineer, visiting Tectron UK for a few days.

The situation

They are just coming to the end of a meeting. Before Peter rushes off, he invites Maria and Jens to his house.

Viewing

▶ 3 Watch Version 1. What do you think they have been invited to?

▶ 4 Watch Version 1 again. How should Peter have clarified his invitation? How should Maria and Jens have responded?

▶ 5 Watch Version 2. Do you think the invitation is now clear? How do Jens and Maria respond this time?

6 Watch Version 2 again. At each of the following moments, stop the video and anticipate what the person will say:

a Peter invites them
b Maria responds
c Jens responds
d Peter explains it will be informal
e Jens offers to give Maria a lift

Post-viewing

7 Peter's invitation in Version 1 is unclear partly because of his use of idiomatic language – 'pop round'. Sort the following advice into two lists, one for native speakers and the other for non-native speakers.

– Don't speak too fast.
– Don't feel inferior to a native speaker.
– Don't let native speakers dominate.
– Don't use idioms.
– Use simple, well-articulated language.
– Ask native speakers to slow down.
– Check frequently that you are understood.
– Don't use language as an instrument of power.
– Remind native speakers that you are using a second language!
– Interrupt and ask for clarification.

Native speakers

_____

_____

_____

_____

_____

Non-native speakers

_____

_____

_____

_____

_____

What do you think about this advice for native and non-native speakers? Would you add any other points to the list?

Language knowledge

PETER *'Oh, by the way, my wife Daphne and I want to invite you to dinner one day this week. Perhaps tomorrow evening, if that suits you?'*

MARIA *'That's very kind, I'd love to come.'*
JENS *'I'd be delighted. What sort of time?'*

1   Listen to these invitations. In each case, say whether it is accepted or declined. If it is accepted, note the time, place, and number of people (if they are mentioned).

Extract	accept / decline	time	place	number
one	_____	_____	_____	_____
two	_____	_____	_____	_____
three	_____	_____	_____	_____
four	_____	_____	_____	_____

Language focus Invitations

Inviting

We'd like to invite you to . . .
Would you like to come to . . . ?
We wondered whether you could come to . . . ?
What about . . . ?

Responding

Accepting
Thank you . . .
I'd love to.
That would be nice.
I'd be delighted.

Declining
I'd love to, but . . .
I'm sorry, but I've got another engagement.
I'm afraid I can't come. I'm going to . . .

NOTE When declining an invitation, an explanation or excuse should normally be given.

Time

Would Tuesday evening suit you?
What sort of time?
Shall we say 8 o'clock?
Let's say 8 for 8.30. (This means you should arrive anytime between 8.00 and 8.30, but not later than 8.30.)

Place

Is it far?
What's the best way of getting there?
I'd recommend you take a taxi.
I'll send / give you a map.

Number

It'll just be the four of us.
We've invited a few friends.
There'll be six people there.
There'll be another couple from . . .

Confirming

So, that's 7.30 on Wednesday?
Let me just confirm that. Tuesday at 8.00, at your place.
I look forward to that / to seeing you.

---

2 Listen to these invitations. Decline or accept each one as indicated below.

    a accept
    b decline (your mother's birthday)
    c decline (away for the weekend)
    d accept
    e accept
    f accept
    g decline (another dinner engagement)
    h accept
    i accept
    j decline (work to do)

3 Now listen again. In the cases where you accepted, clarify the time or place.

4 **Pair work**

Prepare five invitations of your own (e.g. for dinner at your house, for a drink after work, for a game of golf or tennis). Then, in pairs, take it in turns to make and respond to the invitations.

Invitations out

Being invited to someone's home in a foreign country poses questions about what to wear, what to take, and when to arrive and leave (see Unit 5). Going out for a meal or a drink can present other difficulties. It is not always clear from the invitation who is going to pay. Questions like 'Do you fancy a drink?' or 'What about a meal?' could mean you are offering to buy a drink or a meal. Alternatively, they could mean you are simply looking for company. In the UK, we often buy drinks in 'rounds' – one person buys drinks for everybody, on the basis that the next round of drinks will be bought by somebody else. At the end of a meal for which all the diners are paying, we often 'split it down the middle'; in other words, take the total bill and divide it by the number of people present. Insisting that you would like to pay can also be difficult. You hear expressions like 'This one is on me', 'This is my round', 'Let me get this', or 'This is my treat'.

Discuss how these things work in your country. What sort of difficulties could you face when entertaining foreign visitors?

Socializing practice

Pair work

You will find a number of situations described below. Prepare your roles and then act out the invitations. If possible, record the conversations, and play them back to check that you have used appropriate language.

Student A

Situation 1

You are hosting a business conference at your company. There are a number of foreign delegates. One of them (Student B) is the General Manager of a key subsidiary. Invite him / her for dinner in a restaurant. Before you make the invitation, decide on which restaurant, the day, the time, and arrangements for getting there and returning your guest to his / her hotel.

Situation 2

You are a visitor to Student B's company. You will be invited out to dinner. You are only in the country for four days and you only have one evening free (Thursday). Respond to the invitation positively and politely. Make sure you understand the arrangements.

Situation 3

You are in charge of a visitor (Student B). While he / she is in your country, you would like to show him / her some of the sights. Try to arrange a tour of the city and the surrounding area sometime over the next weekend.

Situation 4

You are visiting Student B's country for a training course. He / she will invite you to the theatre tomorrow evening. Unfortunately, you are already booked to go out to dinner with some friends.

Situation 5
You are hosting a sales conference. You would like to invite Student B and his / her partner to a show (a musical) followed by dinner on Saturday night. Before you make the invitation, prepare the details (name of the show, starting time, transport arrangements).

Situation 6
You are attending a committee meeting in Student B's city. He / she will invite you for a drink after the meeting. The meeting is scheduled to finish at 17.00, and you have a plane to catch at 20.00. If you can fit the drink in before your flight, make the arrangements.

Student B

Situation 1
You are the General Manager of the subsidiary of a major multinational. You are attending a business conference at the headquarters of your company. Student A is in charge of the conference and will invite you for dinner in a restaurant. Agree on a suitable evening and make sure you understand all the arrangements.

Situation 2
Student A is visiting your company and you are responsible for looking after him / her. You would like to invite him / her to dinner at your home, if possible on Wednesday evening. Other evenings are possible but not so ideal. If you can, organize the dinner and make all the arrangements, including picking him / her up, etc.

Situation 3
You are visiting Student A's country. You are in the country for another ten days. You would very much like to see some of the sights and you are hoping to do this over the weekend.

Situation 4
Student A is on a training course in your city / town. Invite him / her to the theatre tomorrow evening.

Situation 5
You are attending a sales conference. This weekend you are planning to travel around with your partner. You are not planning to stay in town.

Situation 6
Student A is attending a committee meeting in your town. Invite him / her for a drink after the meeting. The meeting is scheduled to finish at 17.00. You expect Student A will have a plane to catch, so be prepared to offer to drive him / her to the airport after you've been for a drink.

5 Arriving for dinner

Objectives

Communication skills   hosting: time, dress, gifts
Language knowledge   thanking, offering, and responding
Socializing practice   welcoming and entertaining guests

Communication skills

Pre-viewing

1 How important is it to be punctual for social events in your country? How do people dress when they are invited to dinner (in a restaurant / at someone's home) or to the theatre? What sort of gifts do you take when you are invited to someone's house?

2 Read the Video Socializing Context.

Video Socializing Context

The people

Jens Foss
is a Danish engineer, visiting Tectron UK for a few days.

Maria de Miguel
is a management trainee from Tectron España.

Peter O'Donnell
is the Marketing Manager of Tectron UK.

Daphne O'Donnell
is Peter's wife.

The situation

Peter and Daphne have invited Maria and Jens to dinner. Maria and Jens arrive a little late.

Viewing

▶ 3 Watch Version 1 with the sound down. What do you notice about the body language of the four characters?

▶ 4 Watch Version 1 again with the sound up. What are the causes of the hosts' and guests' embarrassment?

5 Watch Version 2 with the sound down. How does their body language compare with Version 1?

6 Watch Version 2 again with the sound up. Why are both hosts and guests more relaxed? How do they deal with the situation? In particular:

a how does Maria deal with their 'overdressing'?
b how does Daphne deal with the generous gifts?

Post-viewing

7 Discussion

In small groups (maximum five people), discuss how you would act and respond in the following situations:

– guests arriving late for dinner at your home
– a guest bringing an embarrassingly generous gift
– arriving at the theatre / opera with your guests, who are inappropriately
  dressed
– arriving too early for lunch

Language knowledge

MARIA *'Very nice to meet you, Mrs O'Donnell. And thank you for inviting us to your home.'*
DAPHNE *'Thank you. You must call me Daphne.'*

1 a Listen to the extracts from eight conversations. In each case, what are the hosts or guests being thanked for? What phrases are used?

Extract	reason for thanks	phrase
one	_____	_____
two	_____	_____
three	_____	_____
four	_____	_____
five	_____	_____
six	_____	_____
seven	_____	_____
eight	_____	_____

b Listen again. In which extracts is something being offered? Are the responses to these offers positive or negative?

Language focus Thanks and offers

Thanking

Thank you. It's / They're beautiful / lovely. (a gift, flowers)
Thank you very much. That's very kind of you.
Thank you, but you shouldn't have.
Thank you for inviting me. Your house is lovely.
Thank you for everything.

Responding

I'm glad you like it / enjoyed it.
It's / was a pleasure.
You're welcome.
Don't mention it.

Offering

Would you like . . . ?
Can I get you . . . ?
What would you like to drink?

Responding

A (type of drink), please.
Could I have a (type of drink)?
A (type of drink) would be nice.
I'd love a long drink. I'm really thirsty.
Have you got something soft?

Declining

No thank you.
I won't have anything, thanks.
Thank you, but I've had enough / I've no room.
I'd love to, but I'm driving.

---

 2 Listen to remarks made in the following situations. Respond appropriately. Listen to the example first.

For example:

'*Thank you very much for meeting me.*' '*Not at all. It's been a pleasure.*'

practice via a role play first, then do the listening activity.

  a You have just presented your host with a gift.
  b A visitor who has been with you for several days is just leaving.
  c You have just finished eating in a restaurant which you chose.
  d You have just given directions to someone in the street.
  e You are returning someone's telephone call.
  f You have had a marvellous meal and have no room for any more food.
  g You have already drunk enough wine.
  h You've just arrived at someone's house and sat down.
  i You don't drink alcohol.
  j You have just given a talk to a group of visitors.

3 Practise thanking or declining in these situations.

  a Your colleagues have just given you a gift on your birthday.
  b Your host has just treated you to a very good lunch.
  c A colleague has offered you a lift to the airport, instead of taking the bus.
  d You feel tired and you are invited out to a nightclub.
  e You have had a very good afternoon being shown round the city sights.
  f You have had a very enjoyable evening at a customer's house.

4 Pair work

Think about how you would make the offers and responses in the notes below. Then practise making and responding to the offers.

offers	responses
another drink	no more, driving home
a second helping of dessert	delicious, accept
a coffee	decaffeinated
a nightcap	delighted
a lift home	no need, have your own car
to call a taxi	good idea

5 What would you say if:

a somebody opened a door and said 'After you'?
b somebody wished you good luck in an exam?
c somebody offered you free entry into a prize draw?
d you wanted to thank somebody for waiting for you?
e you wanted to thank somebody who had helped carry your suitcase?
f somebody offered you a job and you didn't want it?

6

Time	Culture note

Clashes over time can often lead to frustrations. When you come into contact with another culture, there are various aspects of time that you need to adapt to:

a the working day (starting and finishing times)
b meal times (when and how long)
c bedtimes
d waiting times (how patient do you have to be?)
e punctuality (how important is it?)
f socializing time – time for small talk, time to entertain / get to know someone

Use the checklist above to make a brief presentation on attitudes towards time in your country or culture. Then discuss these aspects of time, and any others which you think are important.

Socializing practice

Group work

In groups of four, act out the following situations. In each case there is a checklist to be completed for both hosts and guests.

Situation 1

The hosts have invited the guests to dinner. The guests arrive and are greeted when they ring the doorbell. Follow the steps in the checklists below to act out the subsequent conversation.

Hosts

1 greet your guests
2 take their coats
3 comment positively on their punctuality
4 introduce them to your partner
5 offer them a drink

Guests

1 greet your hosts
2 present your hosts with gifts
3 accept a drink

Situation 2

The hosts have invited the guests to a restaurant. The guests arrive a little early and are shown to their table. The hosts arrive on time. Follow the steps in the checklists below to act out the subsequent conversation.

Hosts

1 greet your guests
2 apologize for being a little late
3 introduce them to your partner
4 suggest an aperitif
5 ask about finding their way to the restaurant

Guests

1 greet your hosts
2 don't accept the apology for being late – you were early
3 one of you accept, the other decline the aperitif
4 thank hosts for invitation to restaurant

Situation 3

The hosts have invited the guests for a drink after work. The hosts arrive early. The guests arrive late and are worried about catching a plane.

Hosts

1 greet your guests
2 introduce your colleague
3 offer to buy a drink
4 thank your guests for help in working on a project together
5 offer to give your guests a lift to the airport

Guests

1 greet your hosts
2 apologize for being late
3 thank your hosts for all their help while you've been visiting
4 decline alcoholic drink and ask for a soft drink
5 explain your worries about catching your plane

6 Dinner

Objectives

Communication skills	complimenting, inclusive behaviour
Language knowledge	showing appreciation, offering opinions, comments
Socializing practice	stimulating discussion

Communication skills

Pre-viewing

1 Do you sometimes feel left out in conversations? Why does this happen? How can you make sure that people feel included?

2 Read the Video Socializing Context.

Video Socializing Context

The people

Jens Foss
is a Danish engineer, visiting Tectron UK for a few days.

Peter O'Donnell
is the Marketing Manager of Tectron UK.

Maria de Miguel
is a management trainee from Tectron España

Daphne O'Donnell
is Peter's wife.

The situation

Peter and Daphne have invited Maria and Jens to dinner. They have just finished dessert.

Viewing

▶ 3 Watch Version 1 from 16.00 to 16.30 (up to Jens's request for decaffeinated coffee) with the sound down. What do you notice about Maria's and Jens's behaviour?

▶ 4 Watch the sequence again with the sound up. In the opening extract, what do Maria and Jens fail to do?

▶ 5 Now watch Version 1 from 16.31 to 17.03. How does Maria feel? What could she have done to enter the discussion?

6 Watch Version 2 from 17.10 to 17.45 (up to Daphne's departure to make coffee). What differences do you notice in the behaviour of Maria and Jens?

7 Now watch Version 2 from 17.46 to 18.30. How do Peter and Jens make sure Maria is not left out?

Post-viewing

8 Here are some reasons why people get excluded from conversations. Discuss them and add any others you feel are important.

– choice of topic of conversation
– lack of assertiveness
– over-dominant speakers
– no opinions / nothing to say

From the host's point of view, the most important skill is to be aware of your guests and their participation in the discussion. Discuss ways in which you can draw someone into a conversation.

9 What do you compliment people on:

– their appearance?
– their work?
– their luck?
– their children?
– their car?
– their house / garden?
– their cooking?
– their intelligence?
– their skills?
– others?

How do you compliment them and on what occasions?

Language knowledge

MARIA '*A lot of my friends in Spain are very involved in local politics.*'

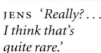

JENS '*Really? . . . I think that's quite rare.*'

1 Listen to these comments made about a variety of subjects. In each case, note what the speaker is commenting on and whether the comment is positive or negative.

Extract	subject of comment	positive / negative
one	_____	_____
two	_____	_____
three	_____	_____
four	_____	_____
five	_____	_____
six	_____	_____
seven	_____	_____
eight	_____	_____
nine	_____	_____
ten	_____	_____

Language focus Compliments and comments

Compliments

That was excellent / delicious / very good.
Well done!
Good effort!
You're looking very nice / great / beautiful.

NOTE
In some cultures, commenting on people's appearance is considered inappropriate, and can be risky.

Stimulating conversation

Offering your opinions and making comments is one of the most effective ways of entering and encouraging conversation. It provides a stimulus for further comment and reaction.

Comments

about a job:
That must be rewarding / hard work / demanding / exciting / dull / boring.

about a film / show / play:
That was terrific / well-acted / absorbing / intriguing / disappointing / boring / awful.

about a person at work:
He / She's competent / hard-working / meticulous / methodical / conscientious / demanding / serious / lazy.

about a person socially:
He / She's easy-going / chatty / talkative / extrovert / has a (good) sense of humour / interesting / good company.
He / She's shy / quiet / introvert / hard to get to know.

about a subject / piece of news:
That's fascinating / surprising / astonishing / incredible / interesting.
It's upsetting / shocking / disturbing / depressing / worrying.

about a joke:
That's funny / hilarious / not very funny / not a good joke / in bad taste.

---

2   What comment would you make in the following situations?

    a   You've just had a very good meal.
    b   You've just heard news of a plane crash.
    c   One of your colleagues is always chatting to everybody
    d   One of your colleagues keeps herself to herself
    e   You've just seen a film which you expected to be good; in fact it was not very good.
    f   A person you've just met says he is an actor.
    g   Somebody tells you a racist joke.
    h   One of your colleagues looks very smart today.
    i   You saw a TV programme about climbing Everest last night. You thought it was very good.
    j   One of your colleagues regularly works a twelve-hour day.

 3   Now listen to the questions or comments and respond as indicated below.

    a   Congratulate her on her win.
    b   Sympathize with her for having such an uninteresting job.
    c   Agree that Catherine is not a great talker.
    d   You saw the film and found the acting very good.
    e   Say you enjoyed your stay and compliment your hostess on the lovely city.
    f   You found the joke about the three Scotsmen very funny.
    g   You think jobs in accounts must be very boring.
    h   You agree that Patrick is always talking and telling jokes.
    i   You heard this very upsetting news.
    j   You thought the play was very absorbing.

4 Developing conversations

In small groups (maximum four people), pick one of the subjects below and then discuss it. Make comments and react to other people's opinions.

a an item in the news today
'Did you hear about the . . . ?' 'Wasn't it . . . ?'

b a record / film / book which you have just heard / seen / read
'Have you seen . . . ?' 'I thought it was . . .'

c a person you all know
'You know . . .' 'Isn't she . . . ?'

d types of work
'I could never be a . . .' 'It would be so . . .'

e jokes
'Have you heard the one about the . . . ?'

5

The role of women	Culture note

In many countries the status of women has improved considerably over the last 50 years. Although there are still relatively few women in senior business positions, many women pursue their careers in much the same way that men do. In the UK , men's behaviour towards women has had to change. For example, men must be careful when they talk about a woman's appearance; some women may find a complimentary remark sexist. Many women prefer not to be referred to as 'ladies'; they prefer the more neutral 'women'. Many women are naturally sensitive about typically male jokes. There are areas of social interaction where men now feel uncertain how to behave. Twenty years ago men would always open doors for women; nowadays some women might find this action patronizing.

Discuss the following questions.

— Are there differences in the way men and women socialize in your country?
— Do men and women talk about different things?
— Do you think the workplace is improving as more women work?

Socializing practice

Group work 1 (for 4 participants)

Choose one of the following topics. Follow the roles on page 76 of the Answer Key.

'Smoking should be banned in all public places.'
'Working hours should not exceed thirty-five hours per week.'
'Private cars will have to be banned in the next century.'

Group work 2

Each of these extracts from editorials expresses a strong opinion about a current issue. Use this as a basis for comment and reaction. Make sure that all members of the group are included. If you find your topic is not succeeding in generating much discussion, move on to another one.

KIDS OUT OF CONTROL

As the end of the 20th century approaches, parents seem to have lost control over their children. Recent research reveals that more than 50% of all 15-year-olds have tried drugs, drink alcohol regularly, and smoke. Despite endless health education campaigns to convince young people of the dangers, they seem to take pleasure in ignoring the advice of their elders.

PLANES NOT SAFE

Recent accidents indicate that flying is no longer the safest form of travel. The ever-increasing pressure to keep costs down means that corners are being cut in the vital area of safety. There is no doubt in my mind that flying is not as safe as it used to be.

THE GLASS CEILING

Many women refer to an invisible ceiling in their careers through which it is almost impossible to pass. It is true that there is a pitiful number of women in senior management positions. Women argue that as long as companies are run by men things won't change.

WORKING HOURS

The process of 'downsizing' – in other words, reducing workforces – has continued relentlessly over the last ten years. One of the major effects of this process has been the increase in number of hours worked, especially by managers. Often they have had to take over the work previously done by now redundant colleagues. Working days of twelve hours or more are not unusual. You have to ask yourselves whether this is an efficient way to run a company, and if it is worth the damage it causes to family life.

TOWN CENTRES DIE

Arguably one of America's most destructive exports to the rest of the world has been the out-of-town shopping mall. Shopping centres, usually located on ring roads two or three kilometres from the centre of towns, have sprung up everywhere. As consumers have flocked to them, village shops have closed and town centres have become full of streets with boarded-up shop windows and 'For Sale' signs.

PROFESSIONALISM RULES

There are few sports where the amateur ideal survives and flourishes. Athletics is nominally amateur but all the top athletes are, to all intents and purposes, professionals. Rugby Union has now officially gone professional and the Olympic Games, the supposed symbol of amateurism, has allowed professional sportsmen like tennis players to compete. Standards have certainly improved, but at what cost? Sport is now seen by many as an activity for a few highly skilled and well-paid individuals, rather than as a source of enjoyment for millions, whatever their ability.

7 After work

Objectives

Communication skills	choosing and developing topics of conversation
Language knowledge	structuring and developing conversation
Socializing practice	conversation topics

Communication skills

Pre-viewing

1 Do you socialize with colleagues after work? What do you talk about? Do you talk shop (i.e. about work)?

2 Read the Video Socializing Context.

Video Socializing Context

The people

Jens Foss
is a Danish engineer, visiting
Tectron UK for a few days.

Peter O'Donnell
is the Marketing Manager of
Tectron UK.

The situation

Peter has invited Jens for a drink after work. Peter feels he should get to know Jens better. Jens assumes they are going to continue talking about the project.

Viewing

▶ 3 Watch Version 1. Why does the conversation not work?

▶ 4 Watch Version 1 again. How do you think both Jens and Peter could have improved their contributions to the conversation?

▶ 5 Watch Version 2. Why does the conversation work better this time?

▶ 6 Watch Version 2 again. What do you notice about the way Jens responds to Peter this time?

Post-viewing

7   Toasting often marks the start of a social conversation. On which of the following occasions do you make toasts? Who or what do you toast?

– weddings
– birthdays
– parties
– work celebrations
– drinks with friends
– lunch or dinner with business associates
– an informal lunch with colleagues
– other occasions

8   What do you normally talk about on the occasions in 7 above? Do you keep very clear boundaries between your personal and professional lives? On what occasions do the two overlap?

Language knowledge

PETER   '*Here's to a successful launch.*'
JENS   '*And thank you for making me so welcome here.*'
PETER   '*It's been a pleasure having you with us. I expect you're looking forward to getting home, though.*'

1a   Listen to these extracts from four conversations. In each case, what are the topics mentioned?

Extract	topics	expressions
one	_____	_____
two	_____	_____
three	_____	_____
four	_____	_____

b   Listen again and identify the expressions which are used to introduce a new topic or to change the subject.

I DON'T NORMALLY TAKE WORK HOME, BUT LUCKILY I HAVE THE REPORT RIGHT HERE SO WE COULD GO OVER A FEW POINTS NOW.

BAR

Language focus Developing conversation

Toasting

Here's to . . .
Let's raise our glasses to . . .
I'd like to propose a toast to . . .

Introducing a topic

I'm glad I bumped into you. I wanted to ask you about . . .
While we're on the subject , . . .
I just wanted to mention . . .
You know you mentioned . . . ?

Changing / ending a topic

Anyway, let's talk about something else.
So, let's leave that.
Changing the subject for a moment . . .

Introducing an 'agenda'

There were a couple of points I wanted to mention . . .
The other point was . . .
There's just one thing I wanted to say . . .

Digressing

By the way . . .
Talking of . . .
That reminds me . . .

Checking and clarifying

Do you see what I'm getting at?
Is that clear?
Do you mean . . . ?
So are you saying . . . ?

---

2 Now complete these two dialogues, using the expressions from the list. After you have completed them, listen to the correct versions.

by the way	*on the subject*	*what you mean*
what's on your mind	*just wanted to talk*	*have a word*
let's talk about something else		

a

A: So, how are you?

B: Fine. And you?

A: Fine. I'm glad I bumped into you. I ———————— about a couple of points. Have you got a minute?

B: Sure. Shall we get a coffee?

A: Why not?

B: So, ———————— ?

A: I'm a bit worried about Stephen. He seems very down at the moment.

B: I know ———————— I think he's got problems at home.

A: Do you think I should ———————— with him?

B: That's a good idea.

b

A: Here's to the success of the project.

B: Cheers.

A: John, while we're ———————— , have you got those documents for me?

B: Sure. I'll let you have them this afternoon. Anyway, ———————— How's the family?

A: They're fine. I don't see a lot of them.

B: Yes, I can imagine. ————————————, did you hear that Michael and
   Kathy are getting married?

A: Yes, I did. In July, isn't it?

3   What would you say if you wanted to:

   a propose a toast to your boss on reaching his 30th year in the company?
   b toast a friend who's just had a child?
   c introduce a new subject for conversation?
   d check people understand you?
   e change the subject of conversation?
   f indicate that you had two topics to cover?
   g introduce the second topic?

4   **Talking verbs**

   Complete the following sentences with the correct form of one of the verbs
   from the list.

   chat   discuss   describe   explain   say   tell   talk   speak

   a He ———————— me a marvellous joke. I couldn't stop laughing.
   b You'll have to ———————— why we need so long for this meeting.
   c He never stops ————————. You can't get a word in edgeways.
   d We need to ———————— the proposals before making a decision.
   e ———————— up. I can't hear you.
   f He ———————— his house in minute detail. I thought he'd never stop.
   g I haven't got time to ———————— – I need to do some work.
   h Whatever you ————————, I won't believe it.

5   **Pair work**

   In the following exercise:

   Student A introduces a subject
   Student B responds and changes the subject
   Student A responds and digresses.

   For example:

   A: *I'm glad I bumped into you. I wanted to talk to you about the new
      department functions.*
   B: *Fine, why don't we talk about it over lunch? Did you see the test results?*
   A: *Yes, I did. By the way, don't forget our tennis game tomorrow evening.*

   a
   A: subject – need to talk about new budget plans
   B: response – fix a meeting
      change subject – met new Head of Finance yet?
   A: response – yes, seems very pleasant
      digression – see programme on TV last night?

b

A: subject – news about restructuring the department

B: response – discuss at next meeting

    change subject – latest results from overseas markets?

A: response – not very good

    digression – hear football results?

c

A: subject – profit bonus

B: response – discuss after lunch

    change subject – Susan's birthday?

A: response – yes, present has been bought

    digression – Susan is planning to leave the company

6

Work to live or live to work?	**Culture note**

1. How many hours do you work a day?
2. Do you take work home?
3. Do you work at the weekends?
4. Do you receive work-related telephone calls at home?
5. Do you mix socially with work colleagues?
6. Do your partner / your friends know much about your job?
7. Have your partner / your friends met your work colleagues?
8. Do you enjoy talking about work?
9. Would you describe yourself firstly in terms of your job (e.g. *I'm a pilot*)?
10. When do you plan to retire / stop working?

Use the questionnaire above to discover the attitudes of friends and colleagues.

Socializing practice

In the role-plays below, each member of the group has his / her own agenda – topics he / she wants to bring up in conversation. Prepare your roles and then record the role-plays.

Role-play 1 (group of 4)

You are four colleagues who have arranged to have an after-work drink, before going home.

Student A

You want to propose a toast to Student B, who has just been promoted. You want to make a little 'speech' saying what a good colleague and friend he / she is. After that you don't want to talk about work any more. You'd like to tell them about your backache and find out if any of them can recommend an osteopath or anybody else who might help.

Student B

You have just got promotion in your job. You would like to talk to your colleagues about how you see the department changing – becoming more participative. However, you realize that this may not be the moment to do this. Be prepared to talk about non-work subjects.

Student C

You are looking forward to a nice chat and a chance to catch up on what's been happening in your friends' / colleagues' lives. You are interested in their families. You would also like to arrange an outing in a few months' time to see a show (musical) together.

Student D

You are not feeling very talkative. You just want a quiet drink. You certainly don't want to talk about work. Your main interests in life are music and sport, and you are happy to chat about these.

Role-play 2 (group of 6)

You are six colleagues who have recently started to work together on a project. Student A has organized this lunch for you all to get to know each other better.

Student A

You have arranged for the group to have lunch together. You are all working on a project. You'd like to start by toasting to the success of the project. Then, as you don't know each other very well, you hope the lunch will provide an opportunity for everybody to get to know each other. Your responsibility should be to make sure the conversation flows. You will need to have a few topics prepared to fill any awkward silences: some item in the news, company policy on smoking, sport, etc.

Student B

You have just joined the company. You hope to get to know your colleagues this lunch-time. You are interested in talking about politics and finding out what your colleagues' interests are outside work.

Student C

You assume the lunch has been organized to talk informally about the project. You would also be interested in talking about work in general, e.g. working hours, the staff canteen, etc.

Student D

You hope this is not just another working lunch. You like talking about food and wine. You also enjoy discussing sport.

Student E

You like talking about music, cinema, and theatre. You hope some of your new colleagues share your interests.

Student F

You would like to talk about work. You haven't been with the company for long and would like to hear more from those colleagues who know the company well.

8 Farewells

Objectives

Communication skills   wishing farewell
Language knowledge   leaving, farewells, reinforcing contacts
Socializing practice   saying goodbye

Communication skills

Pre-viewing

1   How do you behave when you say goodbye to:

– a friend?   – a customer?
– a colleague?   – a stranger?

Are you formal or informal? Do you refer to any future contact?

2   Read the Video Socializing Context.

Video Socializing Context

The people

The situation

Jens is returning to Denmark. Paula and Maria go with him to reception to say goodbye.

Paula Field
is a Marketing Assistant with Tectron UK.

Maria de Miguel
is a management trainee from Tectron España.

Jens Foss
is a Danish engineer, visiting Tectron UK for a few days.

Viewing

3   Watch Version 1 with the sound down. What do you notice about Paula's body language?

4   Watch Version 1 with the sound up. What does Jens seem to expect to happen?

5   Watch Version 2 with the sound down. How does Paula's body language compare with Version 1?

6 Watch Version 2 again with the sound up. Stop the video before the following moments and try to anticipate what is said:

    a the receptionist says goodbye
    b Paula makes a little speech
    c Jens presents his card
    d they shake hands
    e Maria and Jens say farewell

Post-viewing

7 Prepare and give a short farewell speech in the following situations:

    – a colleague is going to take a year off to sail around the world
    – a female colleague is leaving to have a baby
    – a visitor is returning to his country after a three-day visit
    – a colleague is leaving to take up a new position (a promotion) in another part of the company
    – a friend is leaving the area to get married

Language knowledge

PAULA '*I'd just like to say it's been a pleasure working with you. Now we've all met, I'm sure we'll be seeing each other again.*'
JENS '*Thank you, Paula. And let me give you my card so you have no excuse not to call me if you're ever in Copenhagen.*'

1 Listen to these six farewell exchanges. In each case, note whether they have known each other for some time, and whether they are likely to contact each other again soon.

Extract	established contact / new contact	contact again soon or not
one	_____	_____
two	_____	_____
three	_____	_____
four	_____	_____
five	_____	_____
six	_____	_____

Language focus Farewells

Closing signals

*I'm afraid I must go, otherwise I'll
  miss my flight.*
I really have to leave now.
I should be thinking about going.
Well, I'd better be off.

Closing remarks

It's been a pleasure working with you.
On behalf of all of us, I'd like to say . . .
It's going to be sad to see you go.
We'll all be sorry to see you leave.

Future contacts

I hope we'll see you again soon.
*I'm sure we'll be seeing each other
  again soon.*
I look forward to seeing you next . . .
Keep in touch.
Give me a ring next time you're in . . .

Contact numbers

Let me give you my card.
*Have you got my phone number /
  address / e-mail address?*
*I don't have a card on me. I'll just
  write down my phone number.*
You can reach me on . . .
Let me give you my home number.

Farewell wishes

Safe journey.
Drive carefully.
Have a good trip.
Have a good weekend.
See you soon.
Take care.
Bye / Goodbye.

Responses

Thanks.
You too.
Same to you.
Hope so too.
Me too.
So do I.

2   Make a short response to each of the following farewell wishes.

   a Have a good weekend.
   b I hope the sea stays calm for the crossing.
   c See you soon.
   d I look forward to seeing you next week.
   e Drive carefully.
   f Enjoy your holiday.
   g Have a good trip.

3   What would you say if you wanted to:

   a leave because you have a train to catch?
   b invite your colleague to contact you when he / she visits your city?
   c give someone your contact telephone number (you have no
      visiting card)?
   d wish someone a safe trip home?
   e express sadness that someone is leaving?
   f tell someone to stay in contact?
   g excuse yourself because you want to drive home for the weekend?
   h wish everybody a good weekend?
   i promise someone you will contact them soon?
   j thank somebody for the help they've given you?

4   Put yourself in the position of a visitor leaving after a short stay. Listen to
    these remarks made by your new colleagues and respond appropriately.

   a _____

   b _____

   c _____

d _____

e _____

f _____

5 Pair work

One of you is the host and the other is the visitor. Practise exchanges in the following situations. Read and listen to the example first.

For example:

A: *I'm afraid I have to go.* (closing signal)
B: *It's been a pleasure to work with you, and we all look forward to seeing you again soon.* (closing remark, future contact)
A: *Me too.* (response) *Let me leave you my card.* (contact number)
B: *So, have a good trip.* (farewell wish)
A: *Thanks.* (response) *Take care. Bye.*
B: *Goodbye.*

a The host has been showing a potential local customer around the plant.

b The visitor is a consultant who has just attended a two-hour meeting and plans to be back next week.

c It is Friday. The visitor is going to be doing some sightseeing and will be back on Monday.

d The visitor is flying back to America this afternoon after a two-day trip. You may or may not see each other again.

6 Read the text below and then discuss the following questions.

a How important are social rituals in your country?

b How close do you expect to get to work contacts?

Words and meaning	Culture note

It is sometimes difficult to distinguish between genuinely felt wishes and mere ritual. Does your new-found contact mean anything when he says, 'It's been great meeting you. Stay in touch'? Would he feel surprised or even annoyed if you took him at his word and contacted him again?

There are a lot of ritual exchanges in social contacts, from the opening introductions through to fond farewells. 'Have a good day' means no more than 'Goodbye'; 'How are you?' is rarely a genuine enquiry into someone's health. In fact, some cultures discourage real discussion about health, unless you are really close friends. Deciding how close friends you really are is half the problem. Many social signals may be misleading: the use of first names, invitations to someone's home, or a warm hug on leaving may only be the expression of social habits. Misunderstanding these signals can often lead to disappointment or embarrassment.

Socializing practice

Pair work – role-plays

1 You have just finished a meeting with a new customer. You have to leave now because you have another appointment. You want to make sure he / she contacts you to tell you his / her response to your proposals.

2 You have just had lunch with a colleague you know quite well. You have to go back to work. You expect to see your colleague later in the week.

3 You have met a useful business contact at the airport. Your flight is announced.

4 You have been having a drink with some new friends. You need to go back to your hotel to do some work. You hope to see them again soon.

5 You are leaving work for the weekend. You meet a colleague on the way out.

6 You have got to know a man / woman on a training course. You have to leave now but would like to stay in touch.

7 You have just met a rather aggressive supplier at a trade fair. You want to leave and don't want to see him / her again. You remain polite.

Student B

1 You have just finished a meeting with a potential new supplier. You have to finish the meeting now because you have another appointment. You were quite interested in what he / she has to offer. You will try to get back to him / her about the proposal by the end of the month.

2 You have just had lunch with a colleague who you know quite well. You are in no hurry and are hoping he / she has time for a coffee You expect to see this colleague later in the week.

3 You have met a business contact at the airport. You don't really feel in the mood to do business. Suddenly his / her flight is announced.

4 You have been having a drink with some new friends. You were expecting everybody to go on to a restaurant. One of the group announces he / she needs to go back to the hotel to do some work. You expect to see each other again soon.

5 You are leaving work for the weekend. You meet a colleague on the way out.

6 You have got to know a man / woman on a training course. You have to leave now but would like to stay in touch.

7 You have just met a rather good potential customer at a trade fair. You want to make sure you have the basis for contacting him / her again in the near future. You remain polite.

Listening Tapescript

Unit 1

Exercise 7

Extract one

In my country we shake hands every time we meet someone. If it's someone we know, we might hug them or even kiss them. We always pass the time of day, exchange a few comments about the weather or maybe the harvest. We use first names with most people, just people in authority – you know, doctors, lawyers, government officials, then we use their titles, you know, Dr so-and-so.

Extract two

We tend to shake hands the first time we meet, but generally we don't encourage much physical contact. Socializing is not so important; we go through the motions and then we like to get down to business. We use first names after we've known someone for a while, otherwise we always use surnames.

Extract three

Getting to know someone is very important – spending time asking about their family, where they come from, is all part of the process. Shaking hands firmly and for quite a long time is a sign of a real welcome. If it's someone we know quite well, we kiss them on both cheeks. Using first names is very much a question of generation; the older generation don't use them so much, younger people only use first names.

Extract four

We usually bow slightly when we meet someone – it's a sign of respect. We also often exchange business cards. We don't use first names unless our guests insist. We spend time on small talk, but we don't ask our guests intimate questions. We don't like to be too curious.

Exercise 1

Extract one

A: I'd like to welcome you to our Institute. I am Professor Stansilav.
B: It's an honour to meet you, professor.
A: Did you have a good trip?
B: Yes, thank you.
A: Good. So, shall we start the tour?
B: Certainly. I'm looking forward to it.

Extract two

A: Hello, I'm Pete Stanford.
B: Hi. Nice to meet you. I'm Sheena, a friend of Paul's.
A: So, do you know many people here?
B: Most of them. I'll introduce you to a few if you like.
A: Thanks. So where are you from?

Extract three

A: Good morning, welcome to Bond Associates.
B: Hello.
A: My name's Deborah Polovsky, but just call me Debbie –
   everybody does!
B: It's a pleasure to meet you. My name's Susan Denison.
A: So, have you checked in to your hotel?
B: Yes, I have. I've got a great room overlooking the bay.
A: Wonderful. We're having some lovely weather at the moment. Let's hope
   it continues. How was the weather back home?
B: Pretty dismal, actually. Cold and wet. It was great to step off the plane
   into all this sunshine.

Extract four

A: Have you met Jonathan?
B: No, I haven't. Please introduce me.
A: Jonathan, this is Maggie. She works in the Research Department.
C: Nice to meet you, Maggie. How long have you been here?
B: With the company? Oh . . . too long . . . nearly fifteen years. What
   about you?
C: I don't work here. I'm just on a visit for a couple of days.
B: Oh? Where are you staying?
C: Greg is putting me up.
B: And have you seen much of the city?
C: Well, not as much as I'd like to . . .

Exercise 2

1 How do you do. My name's Jorge Rodrigues.
2 Have you met Mary Gallagher?
3 Hello. I'm Marcel. Are you new around here?
4 Let me introduce myself. I'm Georgina Pollard, Head of Internal Sales.
5 Welcome to the Sunset Corporation.

Exercise 4

1 What was the weather like when you left?
   Pretty cold. It was only four degrees when I left home.
2 How do you find the weather?
   Lovely. Sunny skies. Nice and warm.
3 I suppose this weather must be a bit of shock to you?
   It is a bit. It was below zero back in the States.
4 How was your trip?
   Fine. Everything went smoothly, thank you.
5 Did you have any trouble finding us?
   No problems at all. The map you sent me was excellent.
6 Did you get in on time?
   Just a little bit late.
7 How's the hotel?
   Very comfortable, thank you.
8 Did you find somewhere to stay?
   Not yet. Could you recommend somewhere?
9 Have you got a room with a view?
   Unfortunately not. All I can see is the factory opposite.
10 How was the crossing?
    A bit rough, but not too bad.

Unit 2

Exercise 1

Extract one

A: Where do you come from?
B: India.
A: Oh, whereabouts?
B: The south.
A: Interesting. Which city?
B: Madras.
A: Oh, I see . . . and is your family here with you?
B: No.
A: So you left them at home?
B: That's right.
A: I suppose that must be very hard for them.

Extract two

A: Where were you brought up?
B: In Greece, actually. But my parents are Danish.
A: That sounds complicated.
B: Not really. My father had a job as an adviser to the government.
A: So, did you go to school there?
B: Yes, I did. It was an international school and we had to speak English.
A: Your English is very good.
B: Thanks. In fact, I use it all the time in my current job.
A: What do you do?
B: I'm a pilot . . . you know, on a commercial airline.
A: Really? My brother is training to become a pilot.
B: Oh? Where's he training?

Extract three

A: What do you do for a living?
B: I'm in banking.
A: Oh, what sort of banking?
B: Foreign exchange transactions.
A: I see. And have you always been in that line of work?
B: Yes, I have.
A: Personally I've changed my career twice already. I started out as a dentist, but I decided that people's teeth didn't really interest me, so I moved on to become a salesman for one of the big pharmaceutical companies. After a while I couldn't stand it, and now I've set up a garden centre just near here.
B: I see.
A: Right, well, I suppose I should think about going soon.

Extract four

A: Are you married?
B: No.
A: So, I don't suppose you have any children?
B: Well, . . . not that I know of. What about you?
A: Yes, I'm married. We've got two boys.
B: And how old are they?
A: One's five and the other one's three. They're a real handful.
B: I bet. Rather you than me. I know I'd have to give up climbing if I had kids.
A: You're not a climber?
B: Yes. I do a bit. Mostly in this country. You know, Scotland, sometimes in Wales, that sort of thing.
A: Well, that's a coincidence. You're quite right about the family. Until our oldest was born, I was a climbing fanatic. Went away most weekends . . .

Exercise 2

a What do you do?
b How long have you been doing this job?
c Do you like your work?
d How's business at the moment?
e What do you do at weekends?
f Do you like sport?
g Are you married?
h Do you have any children?
i Where were you born?
j Were you brought up there?

(Sample exchanges)

a What do you do?
  I'm in computers. What about you?
b How long have you been doing this job?
  For about fifteen years. I could do with a break.
c Do you like your work?
  Yes, very much. Of course, sometimes it's difficult.

    d How's business at the moment?
       Okay. It's very up and down.
    e What do you do at weekends?
       I usually spend them at home. We try to get out on Sunday.
    f Do you like sport?
       Not very much. Do you?
    g Are you married?
       Not at the moment.
    h Do you have any children?
       No, I don't. What about you?
    i Where were you born?
       In Egypt. Unfortunately, I don't remember much about it.
    j Were you brought up there?
       No, I grew up in Yorkshire, in the North of England. Do you know it?

Unit 3

Exercise 1

Extract one

A: Morning, Anna, how are you?

B: Fine, thanks. I'm glad I caught you.

A: Oh yes? What can I do for you?

B: Well, you know that advertisement for a holiday cottage you put in the company newsletter?

A: Of course. The cottage is still available for one or two weeks this summer if you're interested.

B: Good. Could I see the details and take them home to show the family?

A: Of course. I've got them in my office.

B: Great. I'll drop by later today.

A: Fine, see you later.

Extract two

A: Hi. How are things?

B: Pretty good. And you?

A: Not so bad. How are you settling down in your new flat?

B: OK. I'm in the middle of decorating it. In fact, I wanted to ask you a favour.

A: Go ahead.

B: Could I borrow a stepladder – you know, to reach the ceilings?

A: Should be no problem. We've got one somewhere.

B: Oh, that's good. Shall I come round to pick it up?

A: Fine. What about this evening?

B: If that's all right.

Extract three

A: Hi, John. Lovely day, isn't it?
B: Hello, Catherine. It certainly is.
A: Oh, John, could I ask you a favour?
B: Of course.
A: I was wondering if I could use your car this afternoon?
B: Well, I'm not sure it's insured for anybody else to drive.
A: I'm fairly certain the company insurance will cover it.
B: Well, if you're sure.
A: I'll check first and give you a ring in a moment.
B: OK. Speak to you later, then.

Exercise 2

a

A: Hi, Marion. How are things?
B: Not so bad. What about you?
A: Fine, thanks. I wondered if I could ask you a favour?
B: Try me.
A: Could I borrow your laptop for the weekend?
B: I suppose so. I'll bring it in tomorrow.
A: Thanks, Marion. That's really good of you.

b

A: Morning, Tom. How are you?
B: OK. And you?
A: Actually, I'm feeling a bit rough.
B: Oh, I'm sorry to hear that.
A: You couldn't give me a couple of aspirin?
B: Umm . . . sorry, I don't have any on me. Why don't you try Jonathan? He's a walking medical chest.
A: Good idea. See you later.
B: Bye. Hope you feel better soon.

c

A: Hello. How are you doing?
B: Hello. Not so bad. How are you?
A: Fine, thanks. Actually, I'm glad I bumped into you.
B: Why's that?
A: Well, would you mind if I missed the meeting this afternoon?
B: Well, . . . I'm not sure.
A: You see, I've got to pick up my son from the doctor's.
B: If you have to, then there's not much choice.
A: Thanks very much.

Unit 4

Exercise 1

Extract one

A: What about coming round for a drink sometime?
B: That would be nice.
A: What about you, Judy?
C: Great.
A: Shall we say Friday after work?
B: Oh, I'm afraid I can't. I'm going away for the weekend.
A: How about tomorrow, then?
B: That should be fine.
C: No problem for me.
A: Good. Shall we say seven o'clock?
B: Fine. I'll pick you up, Judy, if you like.
C: Thanks. That would be a help.
A: So, see you tomorrow evening around seven.
B: Look forward to it.

Extract two

A: We'd like to invite you to our house before you return to England.
B: That's really very kind, Mr Johansson.
A: Could you manage Saturday?
B: Yes . . . what sort of time?
A: Well, for drinks, and then dinner.
B: So about 7.30?
A: That's fine. There'll probably be a few other people, but we'll keep it nice and informal.
B: Great. I look forward to it.

Extract three

A: I wonder if you'd like to come to the theatre with us on Friday?
B: I'd love to, but Friday's our wedding anniversary.
A: Never mind. Another time, then?
B: Certainly. It'd be a pleasure.

Extract four

A: Would you like to join us for lunch on Wednesday?
B: Thanks, that would be nice.
A: We've booked a table at Giovanni's. Do you know it?
B: Yes. It's on Market Street, isn't it?
A: That's right. There's a table for six booked for one o'clock.
B: Fine, who else is coming?
A: Let's see . . . you know Dorothea and Charles and Richard, and there'll be a new member of the team – Judith. It'll be a good opportunity for you to meet her.
B: Good. I look forward to it.

Exercise 2

a Could you come to dinner on Friday?
b What about joining us at the opera on Friday?
c We'd like to invite you to our house on Sunday for lunch.
d What do you think about eating out on Saturday?
e Come on. Let's go for a drink.
f We wondered whether you'd like to come round for dinner one evening?
g We're going out for a bite to eat. Why don't you join us?
h How about a drink after work?
i Would you like to come home one evening?
j Do you fancy a meal?

Unit 5

Exercise 1

Extract one

A: Very nice to meet you, Mrs Lenahan. Here's a small gift.
B: Oh, thank you. They're lovely. I must put them in some water.
A: I'm glad you like them.

Extract two

A: Well, we really must go now. It was a delightful evening. Thank you very much.
B: It was a pleasure to see you. I hope it won't be too long before you're here again.
A: Me too.

Extract three

A: What about a glass of wine?
B: Thank you. That would be nice.

Extract four

A: Would you like another drink?
B: No, thanks. I've got to drive.
A: What about something soft – a fruit juice?
B: That would be nice. Thanks.

Extract five

A: It's very kind of you to invite us. You have a really lovely house.
B: Thank you for saying so.

Extract six

A: Thanks for all your help while I've been here.
B: Don't mention it. It's been a pleasure having you.

Extract seven

A: Thanks for looking after me so well.
B: It was nothing. It's been great to have you with us.

Extract eight

A: Would you like some more?

B: Thanks, it was delicious, but I'm afraid I couldn't.

Exercise 2

a Thank you. That's really very kind.

b Well, time to go. Thank you for looking after me so well.

c That was a delicious meal. You really chose a marvellous restaurant.

d A: So, you can't miss it. (*giving directions*)
  B: Thanks very much for your time.

e A: This is John, returning your call. (*on the phone*)
  B: Thanks for getting back to me so promptly.

f So, what about a little more cheese?

g Would you like a bit more wine?

h So, let me get you something to drink. What will you have?

i Would you like a drink? A beer, some wine?

j Thank you. That was very informative.

Unit 6

Exercise 1

Extract one

A: Have you had enough?

B: Yes, thank you. It was delicious.

Extract two

A: What did you think of the film?

B: I thought it was awful. I found it really violent.

Extract three

A: What do you do?

B: I'm an analyst in the city.

A: That must be very demanding.

Extract four

A: He works so hard.

B: I agree. I think he sets a bad example. He never leaves the office before nine o'clock.

Extract five

A: . . . and this guy said to Peter, 'Which way now?' and Peter said, 'You've got the wrong address. You'll have to go back the way you came!'

B: (*laughs*) That's very funny.

Extract six

A: Did you hear the news about the tax increases?

B: Yes I did. Isn't it depressing?

Extract seven

A: She's a lovely woman. She's just a bit shy – it takes time to get to know her.

B: Yes, I've heard that. Is she coming tonight?

Extract eight

A: So what line are you in?

B: I'm a security consultant.

A: Oh, that sounds interesting.

Extract nine

A: Did you see that play on television last night?

B: Yes I did. It was intriguing, but I'm not sure I found it very believable.

A: Really? I did.

Extract ten

A: I got through my law exams.

B: Well done! So what's the next step?

A: A job, I hope.

Exercise 3

a   I've just won a small prize on the lottery!
b   I'm working in a warehouse. Fortunately, it's only a temporary job.
c   Catherine is rather quiet, not so easy to get to know.
d   Did you see the film last night?
e   Did you enjoy your stay here?
f   Did he tell you the joke about the three Scotsmen?
g   He's a bookkeeper, you know.
h   Patrick never stops talking, does he?
i   Did you hear the news about that train crash?
j   I thought the play was rather boring.

Unit 7

Exercise 1

Extract one

A: So, here's to the new addition to your family!

B: Thanks. Cheers.

A: How's the baby doing?

B: Just fine. She's growing fast.

A: And what about your wife?

B: She's fine too. They'll be home in a couple of days.

A: I hope you're getting lots of sleep. You'll need it.

B: That's what everybody says. Marc, I just wanted to ask you about that old boat you have for sale.

A: Sure. Don't tell me you're interested?

B: Well, I might be.

Extract two

A: So, let's raise our glasses to the success of the team.

B: I'll drink to that.

C: We all will.

A: There were a couple of points I wanted to mention, just informally. The first is to do with Sandra. I think you've all met her. Anyway, she's not been too well lately, so I'd be grateful if you could go a bit easy on her. Don't overload her with work. OK?

B: Sure.

A: The other thing I wanted to mention is that we're collecting money for Daniela. She's due to leave in a couple of weeks to have her baby. Five pounds seems to be the going rate.

B: I think I can just about manage that. Here you are.

A: Thanks.

C: Sorry, I haven't got anything on me. I'll let you have it tomorrow.

A: Fine.

Extract three

A: So cheers. How's life with you?

B: Not bad. Cheers.

A: Got any plans for this year?

B: You mean on the home front?

A: Yes, I was thinking of holidays.

B: We're hoping to go to North Africa this summer. We haven't booked anything, but some friends went to Tunisia last year and really enjoyed it.

A: Sounds good.

B: What about you?

A: I never book anything till the last minute.

B: Typical! By the way, talking of last minute plans, you know the meeting this afternoon? Have you got time for a quick chat about it?

A: Sure, fire away.

Extract four

A: I'd like to propose a toast to Jan, who's been with us for twenty years. And who, hopefully, will stay another twenty. Jan.

B, C, D: To Jan. Best of luck.

A: I wanted to ask you, Jan. What's the biggest change you've noticed since you've been here?

E: Oh, I don't know, really. I suppose the office environment's changed a lot. We used to have a supervisor walking up and down, making sure we were all working. Nowadays, there's more freedom, but in some ways there are more worries.

A: I know what you mean. I'm sure there were a lot more staff twenty years ago.

E: There certainly were. Anyway, let's change the subject! Who's interested in going on somewhere to eat?

B, C, D: Yes, good idea. Why not!

A: Where were you thinking of going?

Exercise 2

a

A: So, how are you?

B: Fine. And you?

A: Fine. I'm glad I bumped into you. I wanted to talk about a couple of points. Have you got a minute?

B: Sure, shall we get a coffee?

A: Why not?

B: So, what's on your mind?

A: I'm a bit worried about Stephen. He seems very down at the moment.

B: I know what you mean. I think he's got problems at home.

A: Do you think I should have a word with him?

B: That's a good idea.

b

A: Here's to the success of the project.

B: Cheers.

A: John, while we're on the subject, have you got those documents for me?

B: Sure. I'll let you have them this afternoon. Anyway, let's talk about something else. How's the family?

A: They're fine. I don't see a lot of them.

B: Yes, I can imagine. By the way, did you hear that Michael and Kathy are getting married?

A: Yes, I did. In July, isn't it?

Unit 8

Exercise 1

Extract one

A: Look, I must fly. I've got a train to catch.

B: Okay. Have a good weekend.

A: You too. See you sometime next week.

B: Right. Bye.

A: Bye.

Extract two

A: I'm afraid I must leave now. My plane is at six.

B: Of course, Mr Durram. It's been a pleasure to have you with us today, and I hope we can expect to see you again sometime.

A: Without doubt. Thank you for your hospitality. Here's my card, so don't hesitate to contact me if you're in Delhi.

B: I'll do that. Have a safe journey.

A: Thank you. Goodbye.

B: Goodbye.

Extract three

A: On behalf of the team, I'd like to wish you all the best for the future. It's been great working with you over the last few years. And I hope we won't lose touch.

B: I'm sure we won't – and thank you for those kind words. I'll let you know my address once I've settled in.

A: Good. So, keep in touch.
B: I will. Goodbye.
A: Bye.

Extract four

A: I must get going now. I'd like to miss the traffic.
B: OK. Thanks for coming over. I look forward to seeing the draft report next week.
A: Sure. So, we'll be in touch early next week.
B: Good. Drive carefully then.
A: Right. Bye.
B: Bye.

Extract five

A: I'm sure we'll be seeing you again in the future.
B: I hope so. In the meantime, here's my card. Don't hesitate to contact me if you have any queries.
A: I will. Have I given you my card?
B: No, I don't think so.
A: Well, here it is. Have a good trip back.
B: You too. Bye.
A: Bye.

Extract six

A: Right, I think that just about covers everything. Have you got time for lunch?
B: I'm afraid not. I've got another meeting at two o'clock.
A: That's a pity. Anyway, it was good of you to drop in.
B: Any time. I'll give you ring in a couple of weeks.
A: Right. We'll stay in touch.
B: Of course. Must go. Bye.
A: Goodbye.

Exercise 4

a It's been a pleasure having you with us.
b On behalf of the group, I'd like to say how sad we are to see you go.
c You've got our number, so please stay in touch.
d Have you got everything?
e So, make sure you remember to drive on the left!
f See you soon.

Exercise 5

A: I'm afraid I have to go.
B: It's been a pleasure to work with you, and we all look forward to seeing you again soon.
A: Me too. Let me leave you my card.
B: So, have a good trip.
A: Thanks. Take care. Bye.
B: Goodbye.

Answer Key

Unit 1

Communication skills

3 Peter's and Paula's body language is generally quite closed and unwelcoming. They make little eye contact with Maria. Peter's manner is offhand and dismissive, sending negative signals to Maria, who behaves anxiously.

4 Maria expects to be welcomed by Peter, and for him to be prepared for her visit. Peter should have finished his meeting with Paula before Maria entered; welcomed Maria and demonstrated that he was expecting her; introduced himself and Paula; made her feel welcome by making small talk, offering her coffee, etc.

5 Peter and Paula are more friendly and focused on Maria. Their body language is more open and positive, and they maintain good eye contact.

6 Peter gives Maria his full attention. He makes sure his business with Paula is set aside; he welcomes Maria warmly and introduces her to Paula. He offers her coffee and shows interest in her journey. He also discovers that Maria may well have some useful experience to share with them. Maria will feel expected, appreciated, and welcome.

7

Extract	importance of socializing	physical contact	names	opening small talk
one	seems important	handshakes, kissing, hugging	first names, titles to people in authority	weather, harvest
two	not important	handshakes only with people you know well	first names only	straight down to business
three	important	firm handshake kiss on cheek	older generation surnames, young generation first names	family, origins, etc.
four	not so important	bow	surnames unless guests insist on first names	no personal subjects

Language knowledge

1

Extract	formal / informal	business / pleasure
one	formal	business
two	informal	pleasure
three	informal	business
four	informal	business

2   1 d   2 e   3 c   4 a   5 b

3   These are some suggested answers. Others are possible.

   a   How do you do. We haven't met. My name's . . . I work in . . .
   b   I don't believe you've met my wife / husband / partner / friend.
       This is . . .
   c   I'm very pleased to welcome you to the . . . department. Let me
       introduce you to your new colleagues. This is . . .
   d   Hello, my name's . . . I'm a colleague of your mother's.
   e   Hello. May I introduce myself? My name's . . . I'm in charge of . . .

4   1 c   2 h   3 g   4 b   5 e   6 a   7 j   8 d   9 i   10 f

5   a   It's rather cold.
    b   The room's a bit dirty.
    c   The view's pretty awful.
    d   The crossing was a bit rough.
    e   The traffic was rather slow.
    f   The weather's a little disappointing.

Socializing practice

1   **Pair work**

   A: I have great pleasure in welcoming you to A & T. My name's Johan
      Petersson and I'm the Factory Manager here.
   B: How do you do. My name's Susan Parkes.
   A: How do you do, Ms Parkes. How was your trip?
   B: Rather slow. I got caught in pretty awful traffic.
   A: I'm very sorry to hear that. Anyway, have you checked in to your hotel?
   B: Yes, I have, thank you.
   A: Is everything OK?
   B: Fine. It's very comfortable.
   A: So how do you find our weather?
   B: It's a bit hot. When I left home, it was around ten degrees.

Unit 2

Communication skills

3   Body language: they are uncomfortable with each other, and with the
    situation; they avoid eye contact and both maintain a closed, defensive
    posture, using the menus as a barrier. Maria constantly looks out for Peter.

4   Paula asks closed and direct questions. Maria's answers are short and
    unhelpful. Paula starts talking rather tactlessly about company flats. They
    fail to establish any common ground.

5 They maintain eye contact and a more open, friendly posture, conveying interest and involvement. They forget to look for Peter after a while.

6 Paula asks more open questions. When Maria answers, she makes comments, asks further questions, and responds more enthusiastically.

Language knowledge

1

Extract	successful / unsuccessful	topic / common ground
one	unsuccessful	
two	successful	working as a pilot
three	unsuccessful	
four	successful	climbing

2 Here are some suggested answers.

a I'm in computers. What about you?
b For about fifteen years. I could do with a break.
c Yes, very much. Of course, sometimes it's difficult.
d OK. It's very up and down.
e I usually spend them at home. We try to get out on Sunday.
f Not very much. Do you?
g Not at the moment.
h No, I don't. What about you?
i In Egypt. Unfortunately, I don't remember much about it.
j I grew up in Yorkshire, in the North of England. Do you know it?

3 Here are some suggested questions.

Jobs
What line are you in?
How long have you been doing that?
What are they like to work for?

Family
Are you married?
Do you have any children?
What about your parents?
Do they live near?

Spare time
What do you do in your spare time?
What do you do at the weekends?
What are your hobbies?

Origins
Where do you come from?
Where were you born?
Where were you brought up?

Unit 3

Communication skills

3   Paula behaves in a rather offhand manner. She doesn't show any interest in either Maria or Jens. She should have had some small talk with Maria before asking a favour; she should have welcomed Jens properly. She should not have tried to conduct two conversations at once. She should have introduced Maria to Jens, and tried to develop a three-way conversation.

5   There is more eye contact and all three maintain a more open, friendly posture. They are physically closer and more attentive to one another.

Language knowledge

1
Extract	request	response (positive or cautious)
one	to see details of cottage advertised	positive
two	to borrow a stepladder	positive
three	to borrow a car	cautious

2   **a**
A: Hi, Marion. How are things?
B: *Not so bad. What about you?*
A: Fine thanks. *I wondered if I could* ask you a favour?
B: *Try me.*
A: Could I borrow your laptop for the weekend?
B: *I suppose so.* I'll bring it in tomorrow.
A: Thanks, Marion. That's really good of you.

b
A: Morning, Tom. How are you?
B: *OK. And you?*
A: Actually, I'm feeling a bit rough.
B: Oh, I'm sorry to hear that.
A: *You couldn't give me* a couple of aspirin?
B: Umm . . . *sorry, I don't have any on me.* Why don't you try Jonathan? He's a walking medical chest.
A: Good idea. See you later.
B: Bye. Hope you feel better soon.

c
A: Hello. How are you doing?
B: Hello. *Not so bad. How are you?*
A: Fine, thanks. Actually, I'm glad I bumped into you.
B: Why's that?
A: Well, *would you mind if* I missed the meeting this afternoon?
B: *Well, . . . I'm not sure.*
A: You see, I've got to pick up my son from the doctor's.
B: If you have to, *then there's not much choice.*
A: Thanks very much.

3 These are some possible requests.

  a Could you lend me 20p for some coffee? I don't have any change.
  b I wonder if I could ask you something? Would it be possible to have next Monday off?
  c Hello. I'm glad I bumped into you. I wanted to ask you something. Would you mind if I left work early?
  d Hello, John. Could you sign this letter?
  e Hello. How are you? I wonder if we could start today's meeting early?
  f Hello, Sarah. How are you? I wanted to ask you something? There's a two-day course in marketing next month. Would you mind if I attended?
  g Good morning. Have you got a moment? I wanted to ask you something. Could we use your office while you're away next week?
  h Hello. I'm glad I saw you. I'd like to book some extra holiday over Christmas. Is that all right?

Unit 4

Communication skills

4 Peter is rather casual and vague. He doesn't consider that Jens and Maria may not understand what his intentions are. He should have specified the occasion (drinks, dinner, etc.), whether it is formal or informal, and the time.

5 Peter makes the invitation more clearly and warmly. Jens and Maria respond positively, showing their appreciation in full.

7

Native speakers	Non-native speakers
Don't speak too fast	Don't feel inferior to a native speaker
Don't use idioms	Don't let native speakers dominate
Use simple, well-articulated language	Ask native speakers to slow down
Check frequently that you are understood	Interrupt and ask for clarification
Don't use language as an instrument of power	Remind native speakers that you are using a second language!

Language knowledge

1

Extract	accept/decline	time	place	number
one	accept	tomorrow 7.00	host's house	at least three
two	accept	Saturday 7.30	host's house	a few
three	decline			
four	accept	Wednesday 1.00	Giovanni's	six

2 Here are some suggested responses.

    a That would be nice.
    b I'd love to, but I'm afraid it's my mother's birthday.
    c Thank you, but I'm sorry, I'm going away for the weekend.
    d That's a good idea.
    e Okay. Just a quick one.
    f That would be nice.
    g I'm afraid I can't. I've got another engagement.
    h Lovely.
    i I'd like to very much.
    j I'm afraid I've got to work this evening,

3   **a** What sort of time?
    d Which restaurant do you have in mind?
    e Where shall we go?
    f When do you suggest?
    h Shall we meet in reception at 6.30?
    i Do you have a day / an evening in mind?

Unit 5

Communication skills

3 Both the hosts and guests are rather awkward in the way they sit and stand. Jens and Maria have very defensive postures, and look uncomfortable – when they sit down, they are perched on the edge of the sofa with Peter and Daphne standing over them.

4 The main cause of the embarrassment is Maria's and Jens's lack of understanding about the formality of the occasion. This is because Peter has not briefed them clearly.
Dress – the guests realize they are over-dressed.
Gifts – they have brought over-generous gifts which aren't appropriate and embarrass their hosts.
Time – they are later than expected.

5 This time, everyone is more relaxed; they make good eye contact, smile a lot, and are physically more open with each other. Jens and Maria sit back, looking more relaxed.

6 They are more relaxed because Daphne is welcoming and puts her guests at ease by adapting to the situation. Maria has the confidence to confront the problem of being 'overdressed', and as a result Jens visibly loosens up. Daphne shows her appreciation of the thought behind the gifts, and makes a little joke – 'It's just like Christmas'. Time is not recognized as an issue.

Language knowledge

1 a

Extract	reason for thanks	phrase
one	a gift (flowers)	*Thank you. They're lovely.*
two	a lovely evening	*It was a delightful evening. Thank you very much.*
three	offer of glass of wine	*Thank you. That would be nice.*
four	a fruit juice	*That would be nice. Thanks.*
five	compliment on lovely house	*Thank you for saying so.*
six	help	*Thanks for all your help while I've been here.*
seven	looking after visitor	*Thanks for looking after me so well.*
eight	offer of more food	*Thanks, it was delicious, but I'm afraid I couldn't.*

b

Extract 3 – positive
Extract 4 – negative then positive
Extract 8 – negative

2 Here are some suggestions. Other responses are possible.

a You're very welcome. / Don't mention it.
b It was a pleasure.
c I'm glad you enjoyed it.
d You're welcome.
e No problem. What can I do for you?
f Thank you, it was delicious, but I'm afraid I can't manage any more.
g Thank you. I've had enough.
h A glass of wine, please. / What have you got?
i Something soft, please, if you don't mind.
j I'm glad you found it interesting.

3 Here are some suggestions. Other responses are possible.

a Thank you very much. That's very kind of you.
b That was delicious. Thank you.
c That's very kind of you.
d Thank you, but I'm feeling a bit tired tonight. I think I'll just go home.
e That was really interesting. Thank you for giving up your time.
f That was a lovely evening. Thank you very much.

4 Here are some suggestions. Other responses are possible.

Would you like another drink?	I'd love one, but I'm afraid I'm driving home.
Do have some more dessert.	Thank you, I will. It was delicious.
Would you like a coffee?	Yes please, could I have decaffeinated?
Would you like a nightcap?	That would be nice. Thank you.
Can I give you a lift home?	Thanks very much for the offer, but I've got my car.
Shall I call you a taxi?	Thank you. That's a good idea.

5 Here are some suggestions. Other responses are possible.

   a Thank you. / No, after you.
   b Thanks. I'll need it.
   c Thanks. That's very kind, but . . .
   d Thanks for waiting.
   e Thanks for helping. That was very kind of you.
   f Thank you for thinking of me, but I'm afraid I can't take it.

Unit 6

Communication skills

3 Jens and Maria pay no attention to Daphne. Peter and Jens tend to exclude the women from their conversation.

4 They don't compliment Daphne on the food. They are not attentive to Daphne, nor do they respond to her offer of coffee; they communicate only through Peter.

5 Maria feels excluded from Peter's and Jens's conversation. She needs to be more assertive, and offer her opinions in this discussion, but is not really given the opportunity.

6 They compliment Daphne on the food. They are appreciative and attentive, and speak to her directly.

7 Peter asks Maria for her opinion, so she is able to enter the discussion and expresses herself quite assertively. Jens responds seriously and thoughtfully to her point of view.

Language knowledge

1

Extract	subject of comment	positive / negative
one	food	positive
two	film	negative
three	job (analyst)	positive
four	working hard	negative
five	joke	positive
six	tax increase	negative
seven	a woman	positive
eight	job (security consultant)	positive
nine	television play	positive / negative
ten	passing law exam	positive

2 Here are some suggestions. Other comments are possible.

a That was delicious.
b Isn't it awful / dreadful.
c She's very talkative / chatty / she can't stop talking.
d She's quiet / the quiet type.
e That was disappointing.
f Really. That must be interesting.
g I don't find that very funny.
h You're looking very smart.
i Did you see that programme about Everest last night? Wasn't it good?
j He's a real workaholic!

3 Here are some suggestions. Other responses are possible.

a Congratulations. Well done!
b That must be hard. It can't be very interesting work.
c You're right. She's hard to get to know.
d Yes, I did. I thought the acting was excellent.
e Very much so. It's a lovely city.
f Yes he did. It was very funny / hilarious.
g Poor man. I can't stand figures.
h You're right. He's very extrovert.
i Yes, I did. Wasn't it awful?
j Did you? I thought it was very intriguing.

Socializing practice

Group work 1

1 'Smoking should be banned in all public places.'
A: You feel strongly that smoking should be banned.
B: You feel strongly that smoking should not be banned.
C: You have no strong views but you notice that one of the group is saying nothing; you try to bring him / her into the discussion.
D: You feel that smoking should be banned but you are nervous about contributing to the discussion; you don't say anything until you are asked.

2 'Working hours should not exceed 35 hours per week.'
A: You feel that working should be limited to 35 hours but you are nervous about contributing to the discussion; you don't say anything until you are asked.
B: You have no strong views but you notice that one of the group is saying nothing; you try to bring him / her into the discussion.
C: You feel strongly that working hours should not be limited to 35 hours.
D: You feel strongly that working hours should be limited to 35 hours.

3 'Cars will have to be banned in the next century.'
A: You have no strong views but you notice that one of the group is saying nothing; you try to bring him / her into the discussion.
B: You feel that cars will have to banned but you are nervous about contributing to the discussion; you don't say anything until you are asked.
C: You feel strongly that private cars will be banned in the next century.
D: You feel strongly that private cars will not be banned in the next century.

Unit 7

Communication skills

3   It doesn't work because Peter and Jens approach it from completely different points of view. Peter wants to relax, and get to know Jens; Jens wants to continue with work. Neither compromises, and as a result both of them are frustrated.

4   Jens needs to be more sensitive to Peter's intentions or expectations. This is a social occasion; he needs to be prepared to chat socially to Peter before discussing work-related issues. Peter needs to meet Jens half way, and be prepared to talk a little about work.

5   Jens is prepared to talk socially and wait for the opportunity to talk about work. He brings it up tactfully at an appropriate point, so Peter is more inclined to talk 'shop' later on.

6   Jens responds by answering questions about his family. He also shows interest in Peter's family. They 'make contact' on a more human level.

Language knowledge

1   **a**

Extract	topic(s)
one	new baby / boat for sale
two	overworked Sandra / leaving present for Daniela
three	holidays / meeting
four	changes in office life / eating out

b

Extract	
one	*I just wanted to ask you about . . .*
two	*There were a couple of points I wanted to mention . . .*
	The first is . . . The other thing I wanted to mention is . . .
three	*By the way, you know the meeting this afternoon? Have you got . . . ?*
four	*Anyway, let's change the subject . . .*

2   **a**

A: So, how are you?

B: Fine. And you?

A: Fine. I'm glad I bumped into you. I *just wanted to talk* about a couple of points. Have you got a minute?

B: Sure, shall we get a coffee?

A: Why not?

B: So, *what's on your mind?*

A: I'm a bit worried about Stephen. He seems very down at the moment.

B: I know *what you mean.* I think he's got problems at home.

A: Do you think I should *have a word* with him?

B: That's a good idea.

b

A: Here's to the success of the project.

B: Cheers.

A: John, while we're *on the subject*, have you got those documents for me?

B: Sure. I'll let you have them this afternoon. Anyway, *let's talk about something else.* How's the family?

A: They're fine. I don't see a lot of them.

B: Yes, I can imagine. *By the way*, did you hear that Michael and Kathy are getting married?

A: Yes, I did. In July, isn't it?

3   Here are some suggestions. Other phrases are possible.

    a Let's raise our glasses to Henry. Congratulations on lasting thirty years!

    b Here's to you and the new baby.

    c I just wanted to mention . . . / By the way, talking of . . .

    d Do you see what I mean?

    e Anyway, let's talk about something else. Did you hear about . . . ?

    f There were a couple of things I wanted to talk about.

    g The other point was . . .

4   **a** He *told* me a marvellous story. I couldn't stop laughing.

    b You'll have to *explain* why we need so long for this meeting.

    c He never stops *talking*. You can't get a word in edgeways.

    d We need to *discuss* the proposals before making a decision.

    e Can you *speak* up? I can't hear you.

    f He *described* his house in minute detail. I thought he'd never stop.

    g I haven't got time to *chat*. I need to do some work.

    h Whatever you *say*, I won't believe it.

5   **Pair work**

Here are some sample conversations.

a

A: Have you got a moment? I just wanted to talk about the new budget plans.

B: Yes, of course. Why don't we fix a meeting for later today?

A: Fine. Shall we say four, then?

B: That suits me. Anyway, have you met the new Head of Finance yet?

A: Yes, just briefly. He seems very pleasant. By the way, did you see that programme about . . . on TV last night?

b

A: Hello. I'm glad I bumped into you. I wanted to talk about the latest restructuring plans.

B: Of course, but let's leave it till the next meeting. Did you hear the latest results from the overseas markets?

A: Yes, they weren't very good. And talking of bad results, did you hear what happened in the England match last night?

c

A: Hi. I wondered whether we could have a chat about the profit bonus?

B: Sure, why don't we discuss it after lunch? Did you know it was Susan's birthday, by the way?

A: Yes, we've got a present for her. While we're on the subject, did you know she was planning to leave the company?

Unit 8

Communication skills

3 Paula's body language conveys indifference and impatience – there is minimal physical contact, and no prolonged eye contact.

4 Jens expects a farewell in which he says goodbye properly to both Maria and Paula. He's looking for some recognition of the time and energy he's put into the project, and the relationship between himself and the others. He is clearly disappointed and perhaps offended that this does not happen.

5 Paula's body language is now more positive and personal. Both she and Maria convey warmth, interest, and appreciation – there is more physical contact and more eye contact.

Language knowledge

1

Extract	established contact / new contact	contact again soon or not
one	established	yes
two	new	no
three	established	no
four	established	yes
five	new	no
six	established	yes

2 Here are some suggestions. Other responses are possible.

a You too.
b So do I.
c Hope so.
d Yes, me too.
e Thanks. I will.
f You too.
g Thanks. I'm sure you will too.

3 Here are some suggestions. Other phrases are possible.

a I'm afraid I must go now, otherwise I'll miss my train.
b If you're ever in . . . , please give me a ring.
c I'm sorry, I've got no card. Let me write down my telephone number.
d Have a safe trip home.
e I'm really sorry you're leaving.
f Keep in touch.
g I must go now. I'd like to miss the traffic.
h Have a good weekend.
i I'll be in touch soon.
j Thanks very much for looking after me.

4　a　Thank you for saying so. You've all been very kind. / You've all made me very welcome.

b　That's nice of you to say so. I'm sad to go too, but I'm sure we'll be seeing each other again soon.

c　I will. And give us a ring if you're ever in . . .

d　Yes, thank you.

e　Don't worry. I won't forget.

f　I hope so.

Video Transcript

Unit 1 First contacts

Version 1

RECEPTIONIST: Miss Miguel. You can go up now. It's the fifth floor.

MARIA: Thank you.

PETER: Yes, it looks good. I like the colours. Have we got enough time to promote it? That's my worry. And do we have the price right?

PAULA: More input on the technical side would help.

PETER: That's why I'm bringing Jens Foss over. Come in! (*to Maria*) Oh, take a seat, will you? Shan't be a moment. (*to Paula*) Do you know Jens Foss? He's in our Copenhagen office.

PAULA: I've heard of him but I don't think we've met. Anyway, I'd better leave you to it.

PETER: Let me have the draft schedule by three this afternoon.

PAULA: Yes, I'll get onto it straight away.

PETER: And give me a ring if there are any problems.

PAULA: Will do!

PETER: Sorry to keep you. Have a seat.

MARIA: I hope you were expecting me. My name is Maria de Miguel.

PETER: Yes, I've got your details here somewhere.

Version 2

PETER: Have we got enough time to promote it, that's the worry. And do we have the price right? Anyway, let's leave it there for the time being... Come in!... Hello, you must be Maria. I'm Peter O'Donnell. Welcome to Tectron UK.

MARIA: Thank you. It's good to be here.

PETER: Let me introduce you to Paula Field. Paula is one of our marketing team.

PAULA: Nice to meet you, Maria.

MARIA: Nice to meet you.

PETER: I'm sure you know that Maria is going to be with us for a couple of months.

PAULA: Yes. We should be seeing quite a lot of each other. (*to Peter*) If you'll excuse me, I should be getting back. See you later, Maria.

MARIA: Yes, bye.

PETER: See you later, Paula. (*to Maria*) Have a seat. Coffee?

MARIA: Thank you.

PETER: How was the flight?

MARIA: Fine, only a little bit late.

PETER: Milk and sugar?

MARIA: Black, please.

PETER: Paula and I were discussing the Telcom package. Isn't the Spanish office planning their launch soon?

MARIA: That's right. I was helping to put together the promotional literature.

PETER: Ah. That could be very useful!

Unit 2 Getting to know each other

Version 1

PAULA: Seems colder today, or is it just me?

MARIA: Er . . . I'm not sure.

PAULA: Peter should be here soon . . . There was a very good French film on TV last night. Did you see it?

MARIA: No, no I didn't.

PAULA: So, are you settling in?

MARIA: Yes, fine, thank you.

PAULA: That's good. You've got a company flat, haven't you?

MARIA: Yes, I'm very lucky.

PAULA: Yes, you know they're like gold dust. I tried to get one when I first started working here, but they wouldn't give me one. It's a very odd system because some people have had a company flat for years and they pay peanuts in rent for them.

MARIA: Oh, look, there's Mr O'Donnell.

PETER: Sorry I'm late.

PAULA: Good. We can order now.

PETER: Still, it's given you girls a chance to get to know each other. What shall we have?

Version 2

PAULA: Seems colder today, or is it just me?

MARIA: It is colder. It was on the weather forecast.

PAULA: Was it? I'm sure it's not normally this cold.

MARIA: Still, it's warmer than I expected!

PAULA: Really? I suppose it's still pretty hot in Spain at this time of year.

MARIA: Yes, especially where I come from.

PAULA: Where's that?

MARIA: Seville. Do you know it?

PAULA: No, but that's amazing. My brother's going there to study for a year.

MARIA: Really? Oh, I'm sure he'll have a great time.

PAULA: Actually, he'll be here next weekend.

MARIA Perhaps we could meet up? I could tell him some good places to go.

PAULA: That would be wonderful.

PETER: So, this is good! Sorry I'm late. How are you getting on?

PAULA: Great. Guess what? You know my brother, Matthew? We've just discovered that he's going to be spending a year in Maria's home town.

PETER: In Seville? That's extraordinary!

Unit 3 Further contacts

Version 1

PAULA: Hello.

RECEPTIONIST: Hi.

PAULA: I got a call to say our visitor has arrived.

RECEPTIONIST: Oh, yes, he's just gone to park his car.

PAULA: Thanks . . . Hello, Maria. How are you?

MARIA: Fine, thank you. Are you waiting for someone?

PAULA: Yes, he's just parking his car.

MARIA: Oh well, I'll see you later.

PAULA: Oh, while you're here Maria, I wondered if I could just ask you to do something for me? Oh . . . Mr Foss?

JENS: That's right.

PAULA: Paula Field. Could you sign in, please?

JENS: Yes.

PAULA: That promotional material we were talking about. Could you let me have it by the end of the day?

MARIA: Sure. What exactly?

PAULA: Oh, we can talk about it later . . . (*to Jens*) So, shall we go up?

JENS: (*to Maria*) My name is Jens Foss.

MARIA: Maria de Miguel.

JENS: Oh, OK.

Version 2

PAULA: Hello, I got a call to say Mr Foss has arrived.

RECEPTIONIST: Yes, he's just gone to park his car.

PAULA: Thanks . . . Hello, Maria. How are you?

MARIA: Fine, thanks. How are you?

PAULA: Fine. I'm just waiting to meet Jens Foss. He's over for a few days to help us on the project.

MARIA: Oh yes, from Copenhagen.

PAULA: That's right. Actually, if you'd like to wait a moment, I'll introduce you to him. So, how's the job going?

MARIA: Not too bad. It's hard working in English all day.

PAULA: I can imagine. Actually, I wanted to ask you something.

MARIA: Sure. What's that?

PAULA: I think this may be him. Don't worry about it, we can talk about it later. Mr Foss?

JENS: Yes.

PAULA: Hello, my name is Paula Field. I work with Peter O'Donnell. Welcome to Tectron UK.

JENS: Thank you. Nice to meet you.

PAULA: Let me introduce you to Maria de Miguel. She's from our Spanish subsidiary. Maria, this is Jens Foss from Denmark.

JENS: Pleased to meet you.

MARIA: And you.

PAULA: Jens, would you mind signing in before we go upstairs?

MARIA: Well, I'd better be going. I hope to see you later.

JENS: OK. Goodbye.

RECEPTIONIST: If you'd just like to sign here and put your car registration number next to your name. OK?

PAULA: So, did you have any trouble finding us?
JENS: No. I was sent a good map.
PAULA: Good. So, shall we go up?

Unit 4 Arrangements

Version 1

PETER: That's been a tremendous help, Jens. Really helped clarify things. We'll get these proposals off to the agency, see what they have to say about it. Could you help with that, Maria?

MARIA: Certainly.

PETER: Paula will show you how. Now, I must rush. I've got another meeting.

JENS: (*to Maria*) Promotion!

PETER: Oh, my wife wondered if you'd both like to pop round one night this week. Shall we say tomorrow evening? Yes?

JENS: Yes . . .

PETER: (*to Maria*) Yes?

MARIA: Um . . . yes . . . tomorrow evening?

PETER: If that's all right with you. Right, I must rush. See you later.

MARIA: What does he mean, 'pop round'?

JENS: Probably tea. You know how the English love to 'pop round' for tea. I'm only joking. I suppose it means dinner.

MARIA: What time do you think?

JENS: I don't know. Eight o'clock? Looks like we've been honoured. I wonder whether we should take a gift?

Version 2

PETER: That's been a tremendous help, Jens. Really helped to clarify things. We'll get these proposals off to the agency, see what they have to say. Can you help with that, Maria?

MARIA: Certainly.

PETER: Paula will show you how. I've got to go, I'm afraid. I've got another meeting.

JENS: (*to Maria*) Promotion!

PETER: Oh, by the way, my wife Daphne and I want to invite you to dinner one day this week. Perhaps tomorrow evening, if that suits you?

MARIA: That's very kind, I'd love to come.

JENS: I'd be delighted. What sort of time?

PETER: Oh, 7.30. Nothing formal. Just the four of us. My wife's very much looking forward to meeting you both.

MARIA: That sounds nice. Do you live far from here?

PETER: No, not far. Best to take a taxi, though. Right, I must be going. See you later.

JENS: So that's Wednesday at 7.30?

PETER: That's right. See you tomorrow.

MARIA: That's a surprise.

JENS: Yes. I've got a car with me. I could give you a lift, if you like?

MARIA: That would be nice.

JENS: Did he mention his wife's name?

MARIA: Daphne.

Unit 5 Arriving for dinner

Version 1

PETER: Do come through.

DAPHNE: You must be Maria. It's nice to meet you.

MARIA: Thank you for inviting us.

DAPHNE: Oh, you shouldn't have. Really.

JENS: Mrs O'Donnell, my name is Jens Foss.

DAPHNE: Nice to meet you, Jens. You must call me Daphne.

JENS: Thank you for welcoming us to your lovely home.

DAPHNE: Oh, this is too kind, really. Peter, you should have told them it's only a little supper.

PETER: Ah, not to worry!

DAPHNE: I'm afraid this is typical of Peter. Please, do sit down.

PETER: It doesn't matter. The important thing is you're here now.

DAPHNE: Did you have trouble finding us?

JENS: Not really. Sorry, are we late?

PETER: Drink?

Version 2

PETER: Come through.

MARIA: Hello.

DAPHNE: You must be Maria. How nice to meet you.

MARIA: Very nice to meet you, Mrs O'Donnell. And thank you for inviting us to your home.

DAPHNE: Thank you. You must call me Daphne.

JENS: Mrs O'Donnell. Very nice to meet you.

DAPHNE: Thank you. Please do sit down.

MARIA: I'm sorry. We seem to be too formal.

DAPHNE: Oh, don't worry.

JENS: May I . . . ?

PETER: Let me . . . Thanks. Maria, what can I get you to drink? A beer, a glass of wine?

MARIA: A glass of wine would be nice.

PETER: Red or white?

MARIA: Red, please.

PETER: And Jens?

JENS: A beer, please.

DAPHNE: Can I open your presents?

MARIA: Of course.

DAPHNE: It's just like Christmas. So, how's your stay in England going, Maria?

MARIA: Fine. Everybody's made me very welcome.

DAPHNE: Oh, look Peter. It's beautiful.

PETER: Isn't it? That's very kind of you, Maria.

MARIA: It's a pleasure. They make this type of pottery near my home town.

PETER: Do they? It's beautiful . . . (*offering a beer*) Jens?

Unit 6 Dinner

Version 1

JENS: The point is politicians don't care what the public think.

PETER: I don't believe that. Surely they've got to be concerned? (*to Daphne*) Thank you, darling. That was excellent.

JENS: Mm . . . yes.

MARIA: Thank you.

DAPHNE: Thank you.

JENS: Of course they're concerned. They need their votes.

DAPHNE: Would everybody like coffee?

MARIA: Yes, please. Can I help you?

DAPHNE: No, no need.

PETER: Jens? Coffee?

JENS: Thank you. Do you have any decaffeinated?

PETER: I'm sure we have. Daphne?

JENS: I think a lot of young people aren't interested in politics.

PETER: You're probably right. But whose fault is that?

JENS: I don't know. The politicians' mainly.

PETER: Well, I don't think anything's changed. I'm sure I wasn't interested in politics when I was twenty.

JENS: What about elections? Do young people vote?

PETER: I've no idea. I imagine most of them are pretty disillusioned.

MARIA: Excuse me. I'll see if your wife needs any help.

PETER: I think a lot of the problem is the image that the politicians have in the media . . .

Version 2

JENS: The point is politicians don't really care what the public think.

PETER: I don't believe that. Surely they've got to be concerned.

JENS: That was delicious.

DAPHNE: Thank you. I'm glad you enjoyed it.

MARIA: It was wonderful. The puddings in England are really good.

DAPHNE Do you think so? I suppose we do tend to have a bit of a sweet tooth. Now, what about some coffee? Maria?

MARIA: That would be nice. Thank you.

DAPHNE: And for you, Jens?

JENS: Yes, please. Do you have decaffeinated?

DAPHNE: I think we've got some somewhere. Peter?

PETER: Just normal for me. Can I give you a hand?

DAPHNE: No, thanks, I can manage fine.

PETER: So, what were you saying about politicians, Jens?

JENS: I think a lot of young people aren't really interested in politics.

PETER: I don't think that's true. What do you think, Maria?

MARIA: I think you're wrong, Jens. A lot of my friends in Spain are very involved in local politics.

JENS: Really?

MARIA: Yes. OK, they may be fed up with politicians, but this doesn't mean they don't do something about it.

JENS: I think that's quite rare. A lot of young people don't even bother to vote.

MARIA: I think that's a great pity. For me, it's a sign of a big problem when people don't think it's worth voting.

DAPHNE: I agree with Maria. Everybody is far too apathetic these days. But at least we have a democracry in this household!

PETER: Ah!

Unit 7 After work

Version 1

PETER: So, this is good. Nice to get away from the office. Here's to a successful launch.

JENS: Yes. I'm glad we've got some time together. There was one or two little things I wanted to go over before the meeting tomorrow.

PETER: Don't worry. Plenty of time for that. I expect you're looking forward to getting home?

JENS: Yeah, I suppose so. Look, Peter, you know the question about specifications?

PETER: Can I get you another drink? Try a beer.

JENS: No, nothing please. I need to keep my head clear. I need to go over the figures before the meeting tomorrow.

PETER: Well, if you're sure. Perhaps I'd better leave it then. So, how old did you say your kids were again?

JENS: Seven and ten. Look, Peter, I'd really appreciate it if we could . . .

PETER: Look, if you're worried about the figures, come and see me in the morning. Right, I think I'll just get myself another beer.

JENS: Right . . . OK.

PETER: You're sure you don't want another tonic?

JENS: No, thank you.

Version 2

PETER: Cheers again.

JENS: Cheers.

PETER: Here's to a successful launch.

JENS: And thank you for making me so welcome here.

PETER: It's been a pleasure having you with us. I expect you're looking forward to getting home, though.

JENS: It'll be nice to see the family.

PETER: How old are your kids again?

JENS: Seven and ten. Your oldest, he's a doctor, isn't he?

PETER: Yes, he's doing very well. It's my daughter that I'm worried about – she hasn't the faintest idea what she wants to do.

JENS: I wouldn't worry about that. When I was her age I didn't know what I wanted to do.

PETER: Really? Well, perhaps you're right. Another drink? Try a beer this time?

JENS: I'd like another tonic, if you don't mind.

PETER: Of course not. (*to barman*) Could we have a half of lager and another tonic? Thank you. (*to Jens*) So, what time are you leaving tomorrow?

JENS: I have to leave by four o'clock, if that's OK with you.

PETER: Fine. We should easily be finished by then. And what about this evening? Anything planned?

JENS: I have to work, I'm afraid. As a matter of fact, I have a couple of questions, if you don't mind.

PETER: Fire away. What's troubling you?

JENS: You know those figures we've been looking at for the initial production run? I reckon we've overestimated . . .

Unit 8 Farewells

Version 1

PAULA: So, you'd better sign off and leave your badge. (*to Maria*) What about getting together with my brother tomorrow evening?

MARIA: That should be OK. Later would be better. Maybe around nine?

PAULA: That sounds fine.

JENS: Well, that's it. I'd like to thank you for looking after me . . . I've got my card here. I hope you'll come and visit if you ever come to Copenhagen.

PAULA: I'm sorry, Jens, I don't have a card with me, but you've got our details anyway.

JENS: Right.

PAULA: Have you got everything? Can you manage?

JENS: Yes.

PAULA: So, bye.

MARIA: Bye, Jens.

PAULA: Right, lunch.

Version 2

PAULA: It's sad to see you go, Jens.

MARIA: It's true. It's been nice having another 'foreigner' at work!

RECEPTIONIST: So, Mr Foss. Have you enjoyed your stay?

JENS: Yes, I have, thank you. Here's my badge.

RECEPTIONIST: Well, I hope we'll see you again very soon.

JENS: I hope so too.

PAULA: Jens, I know Peter was very sorry that he couldn't be here to see you go, but I'd just like to say it's been a pleasure working with you. Now we've all met, I'm sure we'll be seeing each other again.

JENS: Thank you, Paula. And let me give you my card so you have no excuse not to call me if you're ever in Copenhagen. My number's on the back.

PAULA: I'm sorry, Jens, I'm afraid I've left my cards upstairs . . .

JENS: Don't worry. I've got your number.

MARIA: I'm afraid I don't have a card, but I hope you'll contact our Spanish office some time.

JENS: Don't worry. I'll send you an e-mail.

PAULA: So, goodbye, and safe journey.

MARIA: Drive carefully.

JENS: I will.